THE BOBBS-MERRILL COMPANY, INC.
3 West 57th Street, New York 19

STRANGE ANIMALS

Pub Date: Dec 12

Price: $3.50

Strange Animals

By the same author

INSIDE OUR EARTH (with Boris Arnov, Jr.)

STRANGE ANIMALS

Helen Mather-Smith <u>Mindlin</u>

Illustrated by Charles Mather-Smith

THE **BOBBS-MERRILL** COMPANY, INC.
A SUBSIDIARY OF HOWARD W. SAMS & CO., INC.
Publishers • INDIANAPOLIS • NEW YORK

Library of Congress Catalog Card Number: 62-19332
Copyright © 1962 by Helen Mather-Smith
Manufactured in the United States of America
First Edition

Dedicated to the
Boy Scouts and Girl Scouts
of America

The Author wishes to give grateful acknowledgment to the Library, University of California, Berkeley, California, and to Mr. Robert E. Hamilton, Head Librarian, Martin County Public Library, Stuart, Florida, for helping with the research that made this book possible.

CONTENTS

INTRODUCTION

We will go on a safari in quest of strange animals. It will take us to many lands of mystery and adventure —to sun-baked deserts, through tangled, tropical jungles, to frozen polar regions and on to the coral reefs and bottom depths of our oceans. Some of the unique animals we find will be vicious and gigantic in size, often without much brain matter. Others that are tiny and defenseless may use camouflage in order to appear ferocious and dangerous or to pretend they are almost invisible. In this way, many animals who otherwise would perish are able to keep alive and obtain food. Our safari will be like watching the fascinating side shows of a big circus!

We will also find some of these strange animals right in our own yards, in a vacant lot nearby or in a city park. Sometimes you may take an expedition just a few feet away from where you live and uncover strange animal wonders.

Remember, all living things which *are not* plants are *animals*. An animal may be a microscopic amoeba, or a blue whale, the largest living thing now on earth. An animal may be a harmless, wingless insect found in the Antarctic or a man-o'-war jellyfish of the warm seas, whose sting is painful and poisonous.

A great many of these strange animals are alive now in our modern times. Or we may have to plunge into prehistoric times and go back millions of years in order to view these animal wonders. But all the weird creatures will be more unusual than anything you might dream of in the wildest of nightmares—monsters with three eyes, fishes that are equipped with swords, termites that have built-in squirt guns, a deadly snake that looks like a beautiful string of beads, and tiny ants that are dangerous cannibals.

You will be surprised at the amazing and wonderful things already known about animals. And *you* will be able to make many unusual scientific discoveries on your own if you will *observe* harmless animals instead of *killing* them.

Strange Animals

CHAPTER 1

Island Animal Puzzles

How would you like to visit a faraway group of islands where you could see strange animals found no other place on earth—animals that have been a riddle to mankind ever since they were first written about in 1859 by Charles Darwin?

Well, there is just such a place—the Galapagos Islands in the Pacific Ocean near the equator.

Here is found the world's largest tortoise, weighing over five hundred pounds and measuring almost one hundred inches around. It is over fifty inches long from the front tip to the back tip of its hard shell. This gargantuan tortoise is large enough for a boy and girl together to take a ride on its back, which should be easy, for it can travel at the rate of only four miles a day.

15

Here on the Galapagos and on no other island or mainland of our globe is found a bizarre marine iguana three feet long weighing twenty pounds. It lives on both land and sea and looks like the frightening dragons of fairy tales or like prehistoric monsters. It has a warty, gray-black tough hide, claws as sharp as daggers, and dangerous-looking sawlike teeth. Covering its head and spine are pyramid-shaped scales.

You would expect such a monstrous-looking animal to be vicious or to spit fire, as the mythical dragons were supposed to do. But instead, it is peace loving and basks in the sun most of its life or quietly munches seaweed, which is its main diet. The only time the marine iguana puts up a fight is during the mating season. The male will glare at another male who threatens his harem; then they both butt their heads together like goats do, until one gives up.

On the Galapagos there are almost no mammals and absolutely no toads or frogs, but there are many kinds of reptiles. Everywhere you hear hissing sounds! The land tortoise hisses as it draws its head and feet quickly into its protective shell. Thousands of lava lizards hiss as they scoot around in the rocks and brush, and also scoot around in the homes of anyone living on the islands. These small lizards have a habit of blowing themselves up with air and spitting if they are angry.

Even most of the birds living on the Galapagos are

Galapagos marine iguana

peculiar. There are flightless cormorants which have lost the use of their wings after years of evolution, the long process of development that takes place over thousands of years.

Of course, there are other flightless birds on our planet. Some of these are the ostrich, the kiwi of New Zealand, and the cassowary found in Indonesia. But only on the Galapagos are found flightless cormorants which are also the largest cormorants on earth. The extinct dodo bird lost the use of its wings, too, and now only skeletons of these birds are found. The flightless cormorant, however, continues to flourish on the Galapagos.

The finches on these faraway islands have variations that make them unlike those found in any other place. And most of the plants that grow there are different from those found anywhere else.

By now you will probably be asking the question, "*Why* are all these unusual animals found only on the Galapagos and *how* did they get there?" This is the great puzzle! As yet, scientists have not decided the HOW and WHY of these animals. But there is one reason that probably helps to *keep* the animals on these volcanic islands—the curious climate found there. For it is this unusual climate which provides an abundance of food.

The islands are set in a tropical climate because the

equator runs through them. The Humboldt current running nearby causes the waters to be fifteen to twenty degrees cooler than the surrounding tropical seas. So there is a plentiful supply of food coming down in the cooler current and mixing with a tropical sea teeming with all kinds of sea food usually found in warm waters.

The barren lava-rock shores abound in crabs and other crustaceans. On the high mountain slopes of the interior, where rainfall is more plentiful, there are dense jungles. From the tall trees and on the ground grow moss and ferns, the food of the Galapagos tortoise.

Even some colonies of sea lions, penguins, and fur seals from the cold climes have taken up residence on these islands. Can't you imagine the leaders of these animal colonies when they told the others, "Let's get out of this freezing cold of the Arctic. We'll go where there is easy living. Let's go to the Galapagos!"

Wouldn't it be fun if we could visit there? Perhaps if you ever did get to these islands and could spend some time in research, *you* might be the one to solve the WHY and HOW of the scientific puzzles on the Galapagos.

CHAPTER 2

A Nine-Foot-Long Tooth

The oceans cover thousands of miles of our globe. Beneath the salty waters are many strange wonders—high mountains, erupting volcanoes, vast plains, deep silts, and acres of rocklike corals, which are the skeletons of tiny coral polyp animals. But the most unusual part of our oceans is some of the creatures found there.

One of these queer animals has a spear jutting right out of its mouth which often grows to nine feet in length. This funny creature is a male narwhal and belongs to the whale family. Its dangerous-looking spear is really a tooth which just would not stop growing. What a fix to be in!

The narwhal, which grows to a length of fifteen

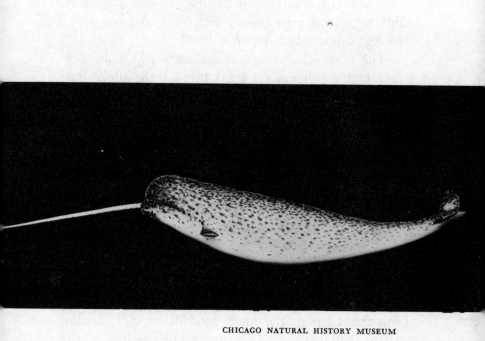

Single narwhal, showing tooth

feet, is found only in the frigid waters of the Arctic seas. It is a mammal, which means that it is a type of animal that is warm-blooded, breathes with lungs and not gills, nurses its young with milk and has hair, though often only a few stray bristles.

The male narwhal has many teeth which are not seen because they never break through the gums. But it does develop two front teeth, one on each side of its mouth. The tooth on the right side stops growing but the tooth on the left side grows and grows, spiraling and twisting as it gets longer and longer. Soon this sharp spear-tooth is more than one-half as big as the narwhal itself.

Now this may sound like an excellent defense weapon and also a means of obtaining food by stabbing it, but just figure out how *you* would go about eating with a nine-foot tooth sticking out of your mouth. There would be problems. And the narwhal must have problems, too, with this lance-tooth. If it impales a squid, the main food of its diet, on the spear, then how does it get the food *off* this long tooth? This *is* a problem!

No one knows exactly *what* the spear is used for— as a weapon to stab and kill its enemies, as a skewer to impale food, for stirring up the floor of the ocean as it hunts for animals that hide on the bottom, or to break the ice when trapped under frozen water.

22

Remember, the narwhal, along with all other whales, must surface periodically in order to use its lungs for breathing air.

There is no record to show that the spear of a narwhal has ever been known to have wounded another narwhal or any other creature of the sea. But one thing is certain, even though the dangerous-looking spear-tooth is *not* used as a defense weapon, it looks terrifying enough to bluff and frighten off its enemies.

Of course, a spearlike tooth may not be entirely good to have. If a narwhal ever had a cavity in its nine-foot-long tooth this would certainly be the *longest* toothache in the world!

There are other creatures living in the oceans that are also equipped with dangerous-looking built-in spear weapons. These are the "billfishes," which include the swordfish, sailfish, and sawfish. However, their "swords" jut out from the front parts of their skulls and are not like the elongated tooth of the narwhal.

Many sport fishermen prefer to catch billfish instead of any other kind of fish because they put up such a good fight, jumping out of the water, twisting, turning, and "tail walking" as they try to disengage the hook. It takes real skill to land one of these beautiful and courageous billfish and many sport fishermen release them as soon as they have brought them alongside the boat, which is truly practicing conservation.

Sawfish

Should you happen to be in Florida or Mexico or the Bahamas or any other waters where the billfish roam, you might get a chance to go deep-sea fishing and have the fun of catching one yourself.

If the odd billfishes and narwhal ever have duelling contests in the deep sea they would certainly be able to put on some exciting exhibitions, wouldn't they?

CHAPTER 3

Live Toothpicks

Vicious man-eating crocodiles, which grow to thirty-three feet long, will attack humans or animals for no reason at all. They are mean and ugly creatures. They have a blackish-colored, horny body and a huge mouth full of dagger-sharp teeth which snap down and hold on to anything within their reach. Both animals and humans are filled with terror when a crocodile gets too close. Everything stays out of the way of this largest reptile on earth—everything except a tiny bird, the plover. This unusually long-legged bird is related to the sandpiper, which is often seen running with lightning speed on our beaches.

The plover hops into the mouth of a dangerous crocodile and fearlessly walks around inside, over the

Crocodile

spike teeth and almost down into the reptile's throat. The plover has no trouble getting inside the crocodile's mouth for these reptiles have a habit of sunning themselves on river banks with their mouths wide open. The strange part is that the crocodile does not clamp its jaws shut and eat the bird. Instead, it holds perfectly still and allows the plover to roam around as it wishes.

While the plover is in between the crocodile's jaws, the tiny bird is getting its dinner. It is picking out and eating food stuck between the crocodile's teeth and is also eating certain parasites clinging to the animal's mouth. The crocodile patiently keeps its mouth wide open while the plover cleans the wicked, sharp teeth. You might call this bird a "flying toothpick."

As the plover leisurely picks up these morsels, getting a full meal inside the crocodile's dangerous jaws, it not only keeps the reptile's mouth clean but it also does another favor for the crocodile. When danger approaches, this long-legged bird gives warning by squawking loudly and flying away. It is the plover's way of saying, "I'm thanking you for the free dinner by sounding an alarm."

There seems to be some kind of understanding between crocodile and plover. The big reptile might be thinking, "Why should I eat the silly bird? It keeps my teeth and mouth clean. And even if I did eat the plover it would only be a tiny morsel. Besides, plovers

Plover

taste awful!" And the plover could be saying to itself, "I'm useful to the crocodile. He'll never eat me because I'm his toothbrush, and no one ever eats a toothbrush!"

This kind of unusual partnership is called "symbiosis," which means the living together or intimate association of two dissimilar organisms which help each other. Many animals above and below the surface of our earth and in the oceans join together in strange partnerships, usually for survival.

The man-o'-war jellyfish practices symbiosis with a tiny fish. The jellyfish has long tentacles covered with

29

poison stinging cells. These dangle below the rest of its air-filled, floating body. And a tiny purple-colored fish lives among the poison tentacles for protection. This fish often lures other fish into the stinging cells. Then both the man-o'-war and the fish join in the feast.

There is a symbiotic relationship between the tickbird and the African rhinoceros. The rhino is known to have poor eyesight, so it allows a tickbird to perch on its back and eat the ticks from the folds of skin. Then, when danger approaches, the bird chirps excitedly.

Humans practice symbiosis, too—there are many examples of human partnerships with animals. It almost looks as if humans are copying something the animals have done for many years.

CHAPTER 4

Mystery Insect

Before you learn about some of the strange insects on our planet you should know a little about insects.

There are about six hundred thousand kinds of insects and they have been on our earth for two hundred million years. They are found in woods, mountains, and tropical areas, in the frigid lands near the poles and at seashores. A true insect has six legs. Thus they often are called "hexapods," which means six-footed. Some insects seem both to smell and hear with their sensitive feelers or "antennas." An insect's body is divided into three parts—head, thorax, and abdomen. Most have two to four wings and, unbelievable as it sounds, they are related to crabs and lobsters. Insects also have a covering of "chitin," a waterproofing substance produced by nature to protect them. But the remarkable thing about insects is that most of them have "compound" eyes. Instead of eyes like ours, theirs are made up of many tiny eyes, sometimes thousands of eyes within one eye.

Among many puzzles of the insect world there is one mystery that no one has solved. This is about an insect found in the eastern part of the United States. It is the size of a bumblebee and is named "cicada," although it is often called the "seventeen-year locust."

This insect does something very strange. It disappears into the ground for from four to twenty years, depending on the species and latitude. During these years it grows from babyhood to adulthood. No one knows exactly how the cicada lives underground except that it sucks juices from the roots of trees and plants in order to stay alive.

Imagine being buried alive for years, burrowing beneath the surface of the earth, twelve to fifteen inches down, where no light ever penetrates. Does the cicada carry on an active, interesting life during all these years? Does it have any fun underground or does it just eat, sleep, and grow?

To begin with, the female cicada cuts slits in the twigs of trees with her sharp sawlike ovipositor or "egg-layer." She pushes the eggs into the slits and, after six weeks, they hatch into little nymphs. This

32

Seventeen-year locust

part of their life cycle is not unusual for most insects go through the stages of egg, larva, pupa, adult or they develop as egg, nymph, adult.

The mystery begins when the cicada eggs hatch and the wingless young drop to the ground, burrow in and disappear. The mystery ends years later when the insect, now a full-grown nymph, comes out of the ground. It climbs a tree trunk and holds on tightly with its sharp claws. The skin splits down the back and the white adult emerges, looking like a ghost with red eyes. No other insect on our earth is so slow in growing from babyhood to adulthood. In fact, a seventeen-year locust takes as long as a boy or girl does to mature.

The adult cicada lives for only a few weeks to a few months. Soon after the eggs are deposited in the twigs of trees both the male and female die.

In the late summer you might hear the steady hum of cicadas. The male makes this sound with platelike organs on its body. And if you look carefully you might even find cicadas just emerging from their earth prison.

The odd life of the seventeen-year locust is a challenge to any amateur or professional biologist. Perhaps *you* may be the one to solve the riddle of the underground life of the cicada. Why not try?

CHAPTER 5

Sea Cow

Long ago sailors came home from ocean voyages and told of seeing, from the distance, creatures that were half fish and half human. They saw them in tropical bays, lagoons, and rivers on both sides of the Atlantic. They said these creatures had fishlike tails, held their young above the water, and nursed their babies. The sailors called them beautiful "mermaids."

For many years people kept a lookout for these mysterious creatures and tried to catch one. Then finally the truth was discovered!

A "mermaid" is really a *manatee*, which is sometimes called a "sea cow." In the Indian Ocean its relative is the "dugong."

Up close a manatee is anything but beautiful. In

Manatee

fact, it is one of the ugliest creatures on earth. It is a mammal, has an eight-to-ten-foot body shaped like a dirigible and sometimes grows to a weight of almost two thousand pounds. Its almost hairless body has a tough hide and a broad tail shaped like a paddle. Instead of the arms the sailors of old thought they had seen, a sea cow has flippers. It uses these flippers to push seaweed and other water plants into its mouth.

As if this kind of a body were not enough ugliness the manatee also has one of the queerest-looking faces in existence. It has small sunken eyes placed in a big, blunt head and nostrils that look like valves. Its lips are thick and pendulous and split lengthwise in two lobes. It has six teeth on each side of the upper and lower jaws and, fantastic as it sounds, if one tooth falls out in front, the rest move forward and a new tooth appears in the rear. Too bad people can't do the same when they lose their teeth!

A manatee is a good mother. Its pup is born under water and, because it is a warm-blooded, air-breathing animal, it must immediately be brought to the surface. Then for several days the newborn sea cow is taken to the surface every three or four minutes. This goes on throughout the night and day. The father often helps out in this exhausting task.

To nurse her baby a mother manatee keeps her head and shoulders above the water's surface, clasping her

37

baby with both flippers. Often a mother sea cow will "baby sit." She will be seen holding a pup with each flipper.

Although a manatee is a mammal, it is helpless on land. It is believed that this homely creature's ancestors were elephantlike land mammals.

When half grown the baby manatee joins a group of others its own age. They are all ready to leave their parents and start their own lives.

Down in the murky depths of tidal waters a sea cow's ugliness is enough to scare away most every other creature—except its two archenemies, the croco-

CHICAGO NATURAL HISTORY MUSEUM

Shark

dile and the shark. The crocodile is the more dangerous foe, for it, too, swims in the same tidal waters as the defenseless manatee. And, if an unwary manatee should happen to swim out into the ocean the vicious shark is always ready to attack and eat it. Otherwise, these slow-moving "mermaids" live a lazy, happy life.

If you should happen to be in the tidal basins or rivers of Florida, don't be surprised if you see a manatee swim up quietly to shallow water or to a dock piling and begin munching its grass or moss dinner. If you are very quiet you will not scare it away. Every time it sticks its head above water to gulp air you will get a good look at one of the ugliest animals in the world.

Perhaps Florida manatees come so close to shore because they know that they are protected by the state with a five-hundred-dollar fine if anyone molests them. So don't get any idea of taking one home and keeping it in your bathtub as a pet.

CHAPTER 6

Ant Dairies and Tiny Cannibals

It is hard to believe that right beneath your feet, just below the earth's surface, there may be underground barns. Yes, barns where there are "cows" that are fed and "milked," but instead of milk they give a sweet substance called honeydew. These "cows" are the larva of the blue English butterfly and they are held captive and "milked" by ants!

When ants find one of these butterfly larvae they all gather around it excitedly and, with their antennae, stroke the honey gland. Tiny droplets of honeydew come out and the ants drink this. Then, in its strong jaws, an ant carries the larva to the underground ant nest-barn. Here the larva is fed on ant grubs and cared for just as carefully as a real cow in a barn. Whenever the ants want honeydew they "milk" the larva by stroking the honey gland. Ants never seem to get enough of this sweet drink.

A certain kind of beetle also makes a good "cow" for ants. These particular beetles, *Staphylinidae atemeles*, often spend their entire lives in the ants' nest and are so well fed and cared for that only occasionally do they venture outside their underground home. These beetles give off a sweet substance and the ants drink this just as they do the honeydew of the butterfly larva.

The most peculiar part of this unusual ant-beetle partnership is the way the ants feed their captive "cows." If a beetle is hungry an ant regurgitates on the beetle's lower lip. This is not very nice to think about, but indeed, it is a novel way of being fed. Another strange part of the ant-beetle symbiotic relationship in the underground nest is the way the ants play nurse-maid to the larvae of the beetle. They wash the baby beetles just as they do their own ant babies. Only most of the beetle larvae die from all this rough treatment.

Another kind of "cows" of ants may be *aphids*, or plant lice. Aphids live by sucking out the juices of plants. In doing this, the aphids absorb a great deal more sugar than they are able to use, so they store this extra sugar in tubes on their abdomens. With their feelers ants stroke the aphids and "milk" them, drink-

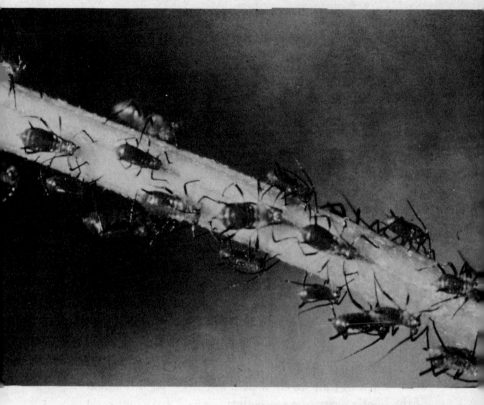

Aphids

ing the aphids' honeydew. Of course farmers hate aphids and they spread insecticides to get rid of these destructive plant lice, for if they did not, crops would be ruined. But ants love the aphids.

During the winter when ants are unable to find plant lice, larva, and beetles to obtain their honeydew, they have figured out a most amazing way of storing and keeping their honeydew fresh during these months. Instead of using bottles and refrigeration to keep their sweets as we do, the ants themselves act as bottles! Certain members of the ant colony hang from the roof of the nest. Then they are fed honeydew by the other ants until they swell up and are about to pop. All through the long winter these "bottle ants" give honeydew to the other ants every time they are stroked.

Humans depend upon getting honey from the hives of bees and are often stung in the process, but ants are certainly clever about the way they obtain *their* honey.

By this time your curiosity is probably aroused and you want to know more about these remarkable little animals that are such pests, always running around under your feet and forever getting into the food on picnics.

There are many kinds of ants. All ants are "social." This means that they divide up various jobs and chores among themselves. In one ant colony you will find that among many workers there are farmers, nurse-

Worker major of the army ant

maids, soldiers, policemen, carpenters, undertakers, and even slave ants. Every ant has a certain task and cooperates with the other ants in an organized way. With this one-hundred-percent teamwork ants are able to accomplish amazing tasks in spite of their tiny size. There are only four groups of insects that are social—ants, termites, and certain species of bees and wasps.

The terrors of the ant world are the army or driver ants which live, among other places, in Africa, Brazil and the Far East. As many as twenty million of these carnivorous ants will start on one of their nomadic journeys—and beware if anything gets in their way! They have been known to invade homes and to suffocate people by crawling into their mouths and nostrils. And they sometimes bite humans and animals to death.

Army ants march at night. Every living thing gets out of the way of these terrifying, destructive cannibals. Lizards, insects, snakes and all small animals run as fast as they can in fear for their lives, for they well know the savagery and superb army tactics of these ants. The army moves slowly along the ground, swarming over plants, searching for food, until they come to a strategic spot where fleeing insects must cross a clearing. Then, as if a general gave the order, the whole army of ants will split, surround the insects and devour them.

45

Army ants have another terrifying habit. As there
is only one queen allowed in an army, any others that
are born are killed in a most savage way. The extra
queens are *sealed* up, then abandoned—they are left
to die as the army marches on.

The way sometimes gets rough as army ants march.
There may be hollows or ravines in their path. They
solve this problem in a most unusual way. Thousands
of worker ants may pile on top of one another, filling the
hollows, or they may even make a bridge with their own
bodies. In this way, the other ants are able to continue
their journey, uninterrupted, as they forge forward.

Another strange thing that army ants do is to use
their own bodies to build themselves into a big nest of
many rooms. The other ants take shelter inside these
"ant rooms." It must be a funny sight to see the walls
fall apart when the worker ants join the others as they
all march on once again.

There is one other species of ant, called an "umbrella ant," which does something no other animal on
earth can do. They grow a strange fungus for food in
their own underground plantations. These ants live
in South America and their nests are mounds of earth
pyramided several feet high. The entrances are large
enough for a snake to use—if a snake wanted to, which
it probably does not. Underground tunnels and cham-
bers spread out in all directions from this mound.

Umbrella ant (painting by Lynn Bogue Hunt)

STRANGE ANIMALS

Umbrella ants are such excellent engineers that even ten feet down in the ground their tunnels are air conditioned by tiny shafts going up to the surface.

The queer part about umbrella ants is the way they grow their food right in their nests. First they go out on a hunt for leaves. With their sharp, scissorslike jaws they are able to strip a tree clean of leaves in a very short time. Then each ant holds the cut leaf over its head like an umbrella, and starts back to the nest. Often the nest is a mile away and a leaf, for a tiny ant, is as heavy as if you were carrying a load of bricks on your back one hundred miles.

Waiting inside the nest are worker ants which chew up the leaves. Next, the farmer ants plant the leaf pieces, cultivating and fertilizing them. Soon a fungus forms on the bits of leaves. The liquid in this fungus is food for both adult and baby ants. In fact, umbrella ants are not able to eat anything else. They would probably die if they ate the same food as other ants.

Ants sometimes serve man. The Guina Indians use ants as surgical clips to help heal wounds. This is done in an amazing way. Giant atta ants are held over the wound and they sink their mandibles (biting jaws) into the flesh on both sides of the cut. In this way, the torn flesh is held together almost as if a surgeon had stitched it in place.

CHAPTER 7

Lazy Birds

There are lazy animals as well as lazy people all over the world, but probably the most extreme laziness is shown by two kinds of birds that will not even bother to hatch their own eggs after they lay them.

The brown-headed cowbird, smallest member of the blackbird family, gets its name because it stays in pastures and eats insects stirred up by cows. This bird has the habit of laying one or more eggs in the nests of other birds. Sometimes the eggs are deposited in the nest of the little yellow warbler. The warbler works hard to build its strong nest, making it out of grasses and plant fibers put together in several layers. Then a cowbird comes along and, while the warbler is absent, lays its eggs in this fine nest. But the warbler is not

Cowbird

always fooled. If she knows the strange eggs are not her own she proceeds to build another layer of nest right on top of the cowbird's eggs.

But some warblers are extremely dumb. They will sit on the intruder's eggs, along with their own. The cowbird's eggs hatch in ten days—which is much sooner than most other birds' eggs, and imagine the surprise the foster mother gets when she sees strange baby birds that are certainly not her own. But some birds are just as tender-hearted as humans when it comes to helpless babies, so the foster mother bird goes right ahead and raises the young cowbirds along with her own babies. The only trouble with this arrangement is that the cowbird babies, with a several-day head start, take away the food from the baby birds that rightfully belong in the nest.

The slim brown and white cuckoo bird also has the lazy habit of laying its eggs in the nests of other birds and not hatching them herself. But all does not go smoothly when there is a baby cuckoo in a foster mother bird's nest. As soon as the cuckoo hatches it pushes all the foster brothers and sisters out of the nest. In this way the young cuckoo gets all the food the foster mother bird brings home.

The most unusual thing about these mother birds is that when they return and find their own babies out of the nest, squeaking and trying to tell her they have been pushed out, she pays no attention to them. Instead, the silly bird goes right ahead feeding and caring for the cuckoo baby. She completely ignores her own helpless babies and leaves them to die on the ground.

How do you think *your* mother would feel if a baby sitter pushed your brothers and sisters out of your house and brought in her own family instead? Your mother certainly would not stand by calmly and do nothing at all. Indeed not! She would rescue her own children, bring them back into their own house, then would probably take care of the children of both families, don't you think?

CHAPTER 8

Warrior Animals

About two hundred millon years ago, long before
man existed, our earth was overrun with huge monsters. At that time the climate on most of our planet was
tropical or subtropical and in the jungles and swamps
lived strange creatures that are now extinct. This pe-
riod was called the Age of Reptiles. If *you* had lived
then you probably would have been very frightened
at some of the awesome giants of the animal kingdom.
Among them were dinosaurs that weighed as much as
fifty tons—the vicious *Tyrannosaurus*, a flesh eater,
that had jaws four feet long which were full of dangerous, sharp teeth. There were also tiny dinosaurs no
higher than twelve inches that hopped along like birds.
These were timid and docile and spent their lives in

terror of being eaten or trampled on by the gigantic dinosaurs.

Would you believe that the fifty-ton dinosaurs and the tiny ones, too, first began life just like a chicken— inside an egg? Only, of course, the egg was much larger. All dinosaurs were short on brains. In spite of their huge bodies they had brains about the size of a golf ball. Perhaps if they had had more brain matter they would not all be extinct today.

Among all the strange beasts of the past was one equipped by nature with a fantastic weapon. This mammal, now extinct, was a *glyptodont*. It had a built-in instrument for defense. On the tip of its tail was a spiked ball! Its long tail looked like a war club, the kind of wicked club used by primitive hunters. Perhaps, ancient man got the idea for clubs from the *glyptodonts*.

Besides having a spiked tail, *glyptodont* was as big as an ox and its whole body was covered with a protective, hard, armorlike plate. In spite of all these natural weapons of defense, the *glyptodonts* became extinct seventy million years ago, along with about five thousand species of dinosaurs that lived in the Age of Reptiles.

You will not be able to find a prehistoric *glyptodont* now, but there is a relative of the ancient club-tailed monster that you can find. This is an armadillo.

Glyptodont

But don't think you are going on a big-game hunt, for armadillos grow only to thirty inches in length and weigh about fifteen pounds. One species lives in South America, and another in Texas and many southern parts of the United States.

An armadillo is one of the oddest mammals in existence. It is completely covered with bony plates, except for its ears and legs. When it is frightened, it burrows

55

Armadillo

into the ground, hides in thorny bushes or crouches beneath its shell. It has a long, sticky tongue that is used to catch insects. Armadillos also eat snakes and roots. And here is something very odd about them— every litter produces four babies and these are always either all four boys or all four girl armadillos. The babies' skin is like soft leather. It is only when an armadillo is fully grown that it gets its hard coat of armor.

If you want to find an armadillo, do your hunting at night with a flashlight, for most of its activity takes place after dark. And if you find one, don't worry, for an armadillo *does not* have the war-club tail of its ancestor, the *glyptodont*. Somewhere along the million years of evolution the spiked tail was lost. And it's a good thing it was lost; otherwise an armadillo's tail would swish wildly, mauling and killing anything that got in its way, just as the ancient *glyptodont's* used to do.

CHAPTER 9

Masquerading Animals

Almost every animal is equipped with a way to defend and protect itself. Some have claws, teeth, stings or horns. Others use speed in order to get away from enemies. Some are so bad tasting that any predator that eats them once will never bother them again. There are still other animals that depend entirely upon camouflage for defense—they look just like their surroundings, and their protective coloring enables them to escape danger. Both land and sea animals have many remarkable methods of camouflage.

The stonefish found in Australia and the South Seas has deadly poison spines on its back, but it blends so well with the coral, where it makes its home, that it can hardly be detected. It has warty, wrinkled, loose skin all over its body, making it appear to be rocklike coral. Its sharp spines are hidden in the folds of loose skin. Often, the unsuspecting step on the back of the stonefish and the dangerous spines inject their deadly poison into the victim.

The diamondback rattlesnake is also perfectly camouflaged with the sand, rocks, and leaves. An enemy may pass right by a rattler and not even see it. But if the intruder gets *too* close, the rattler strikes in self-defense, injecting poison from its hollow fang-teeth.

The octopus uses a very original means of camouflage and protection. When frightened, it expels an inky black "smoke" screen in the ocean waters. In this way it is able to slip away from an enemy behind the thick clouds of "ink."

A three-toed sloth, hanging on to a tree in a South American jungle, has a very peculiar way of camouflaging itself from enemies. In the coarse hair of its body grow tiny plants called algae. In the rainy season this algae turns green, making the sloth look like the leaves of the tree. In the dry season the algae turns brown like the dried, brown leaves of the tree. The sloth is so extremely slow-moving that it is lucky nature has provided it with this unusual means of protective camouflage.

Among other animal camouflage artists there is one, a green caterpillar, that clings to the underpart of a

Three-toed sloth

leaf. No one but an expert would ever know that this blue-green caterpillar with the stripes around its body was anything but just another part of the green leaf.

There is a "stick caterpillar" which feeds at night and spends the day practicing camouflage. Rigid and perfectly still, it sticks straight out from the limb of a tree. It looks like just another twig, so other animals do not molest it.

For the purpose of camouflage most animals have dark backs and light underparts. If an animal had the same coloration all over its body there would always be a dark shadow along its belly, which would make it easier for an enemy to see it. So, whether it is a tiny shrew weighing an ounce or whether it is a mammoth whale, the largest animal on our earth, their underparts are always lighter than their backs. But in Egypt there lives a very odd kind of catfish that swims *upside down*. For some unexplained reason, this catfish enjoys floating on its back. Now, this somewhat mixed up the rule of darker on back and lighter on the underparts. So what do you think nature did to take care of this upside-down swimming catfish? You guessed it! This catfish has a *dark belly* and a *white back*.

One of the most unusual forms of animal camouflage is found on the lantern bug. When it flies, it shows up the huge marks on its hind wings which look like glaring, fearful eyes. Its head looks like a horrible

Halloween mask, the kind that scares everyone. The lantern bug's head has a long, hollow frontpiece with black spots and protrusions which look like a small alligator's head complete with bulging eyes, long jaws and jagged teeth. As if this were not enough to frighten off predators, the lantern bug's body is coated with a waxlike substance that makes it taste awful.

During times of war humans have borrowed ideas of camouflage from certain animals. Buildings and trucks have been painted, and soldiers' uniforms dyed so that they all blend in with their surroundings of trees or desert. There have even been times in history when whole armies have copied the method certain crabs use for camouflaging themselves. These crabs place sponges and algae on their backs so that they look just like the ocean floor. And the "copy cat" soldiers, in ancient wars, carried branches of trees so that, from the distance, their ranks looked like a green forest. In this way, the soldiers were able to creep up close, without being discovered, as they advanced on their enemies.

There are many wonderful things already learned from animals and there are even still more interesting things to find out. That is why it is a good idea to keep your eyes open so that you may observe and learn from them. Then you will have the fun of many exciting, new discoveries of your own.

62

CHAPTER 10

Poison Beads

If you happen to be in the southern part of the United States and should see something very attractive lying on the ground with shiny red, yellow and black bands, your first thought would probably be, "I've found a beautiful string of beads!" But DON'T pick it up. For it may be a coral snake and its bite is deadly! The poison in its fangs causes paralysis and kills in minutes unless antitoxin is used quickly.

Coral snakes belong to the dangerous cobra family of reptiles found in Africa, India and Asia, and are highly poisonous. When they are found in the Western Hemisphere they may grow to five feet in length but are usually about eighteen inches long. Most coral snakes are banded in yellow, black and red, but they

FLORIDA GAME & FRESH WATER FISH COMMISSION

Coral snake

may be entirely black. They feed on lizards and other snakes and lay two to four eggs. Like all poisonous vipers, the coral snake has fangs which are actually hollow teeth pointed backward. When it bites, the poison runs through the hollow fangs and pours into the open wound of the victim.

You might wonder how to tell a dangerous coral snake from a harmless scarlet king snake. They both look very much alike, with red, black and yellow bands on their body. Take a quick look from a distance. Then you will learn the secret, for the coral snake's red bands are always separated from the black bands by yellow. Here is a poem which will help you.

> Red touch yellow, kill the fellow
> Red touch black, venom lack.

It is important to know that a coral snake will only bite when stepped on or touched. So, be sure *not* to pick up that attractive thing which looks like a string of beads.

Now that you know about a deadly small snake you might be interested to learn about an equally dangerous large snake. The anaconda, a member of the boa constrictor family of snakes of South American swamps, reaches a length of thirty feet and can easily swallow a whole pig in one gulp. This snake kills its prey in an odd way. It hugs it to death! It throws its

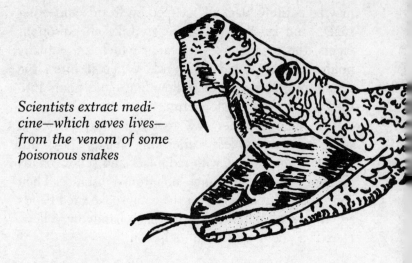

Scientists extract medicine—which saves lives—from the venom of some poisonous snakes

huge body around the victim and squeezes its coils tighter and tighter until the helpless animal can no longer breathe.

Although anacondas live only in South America, there have been several found in the swampy, wild undergrowth of the Florida Everglades. No one has, as yet, explained how these huge snakes happen to be thousands of miles from their own home in South America. Did they swim from distant shores? Did they come into the United States in some sort of cargo? Did they float to Florida on logs? Or did they escape from a circus? Here is an animal mystery that has never been solved. Perhaps *you* can figure it out.

66

CHAPTER 11

Odd Moth

On the Sahara desert of Africa, the Gobi desert of Asia and the Great American desert of the United States, there are vast stretches of barren land where the wind has piled up the sand into hills or dunes—where blinding windstorms can sandblast the paint off cars or anything else in the way, and where there is very little rainfall to wet the parched earth. The animals that inhabit the hot, dry deserts of our world must live in certain ways in order to exist in these arid lands. They are able to do without much water, they hide during the day when the sun is hot, and they come out at sundown to hunt for food.

Even the plants growing there are especially fitted for desert living. They have long roots so that they are able to get water from deep in the ground or they may store water in their leaves or stems.

Sometimes plants and animals work together in order to keep alive on the desert. One of these unusual partnerships is between the yucca plant and the yucca moth.

The female of the species of the yucca moth spends the hot desert days sleeping in the yucca plant flower when it blooms. In the evening, she flies from one yucca plant to another gathering pollen. This moth has no "pollen basket" as do bees, in which to carry this pollen, so what do you think she does with it? She rolls the pollen into a ball and carries it under her *chin*. When she has gone from flower to flower until this pollen ball has become bigger than her own head, she is a funny-looking sight. She can hardly fly as she carries the ball.

Finally, the moth stops at a flower on a yucca plant and makes a hole in the pistil—the seed-bearing organ in the center of the flower. Then, with her egg tube, she drops several eggs into this opening. Next she stuffs her ball of pollen into the hole along with her eggs. In this way, the female yucca moth performs two functions. She fertilizes the yucca plant so that it can form seeds and these seeds provide food for the caterpillars, which will hatch from the yucca moth larvae. There will be enough seed-food for the baby moths

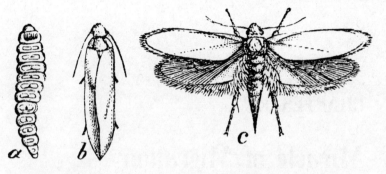

*Yucca moth: (a) larva; (b) moth with closed wings;
(c) with wings expanded*

to eat until they are able to fly out into the desert night
and forage for themselves.

The female moth does not stop after depositing just
several eggs. She has many more to lay and only stops
when she knows they are all safely deposited in the
yucca flower where they will get the proper start in
life. The odd part of this plant-animal partnership is
that yucca plants are only fertilized by yucca moths
and yucca moths eat only the seeds of the yucca plant
—they are unable to digest anything else.

So you see, the yucca plant would die without the
help of the yucca moth and her ball of pollen. And the
yucca moth would die if there were no yucca plant
seeds to eat. This is a very interesting example of working together, symbiosis, and the wonders of nature's
plan for survival.

69

CHAPTER 12

Miracle of Migration

One dark night in 1942 an airplane collided with a flock of swans that were flying high in the air. Two of the swans went right through the metal propeller and another bird jammed the rudders. The plane went down and, of course, the birds were killed.

In the same year there was another disaster when a great many planes on a bombing mission collided with a flock of birds. Some of these planes were so badly damaged that they had to return to their base.

These are only two of the true stories of accidents in the air between planes and many kinds of birds— bats, starlings, sparrows, and others. If a pilot happens to be in the path of these enormous flocks of birds, which often run into the thousands, it may be more dangerous than lightning or storms. It could mean disaster for some of the birds and for the plane, too!

These huge flocks of birds are migrating. Migration is periodic travel from one climate or feeding ground to another at certain times of the year. The birds have their own bird highways in the sky which are called "flyways." Although some birds are stay-at-homes, especially those living in warm climes, others, with only their wings to carry them, travel thousands of miles each year. They have summer homes and winter homes, each in different parts of the world. Plovers, swallows, herons, terns, ducks, geese, sandpipers and many, many other kinds of birds shuttle back and forth between the far north and the tropics or between other long-distance points on our planet. Some of these birds do their flying in the daytime, others during the dark of night. All of them are so anxious to get home that they bump and slam into most anything in their way. The Empire State Building of New York City, one hundred and two stories high, each year is responsible for the deaths of hundreds of migrating birds.

Now, if you were to start for Africa or the Arctic from where you live, how would you find your way? You know the general direction of these faraway places but how would *you* be able to arrive in about the same locale each year just as the birds do every time they migrate? Birds do not have charts, maps or a compass, nor do they have a leader. Each bird navigates entirely for itself. Perhaps you think they remember the way over mountains and oceans, through blinding rainstorms and fog each year. But what about the young birds who are making the trip for the first time? How do you think *they* find their way? Well, the migration of birds is one of the most baffling and remarkable mysteries of nature. Fantastic feats of travel are performed by birds every year.

Except for getting out of the cold, just *why* do birds migrate? While traveling, many of them get killed by storms, enemies and exhaustion. Why, then, don't *all* birds find a nice warm area and stay there year around?

Do the migrating birds have tiny maps of the world and heavens built inside their feathered heads? Or could it be a kind of built-in radar system which gives them such an uncanny sense of direction. Some ornithologists—scientists who study birds—believe that night-flying birds follow the stars for, when it is foggy and the stars are obscured, the birds become confused and lose their way. And those birds who migrate during daylight are believed to follow the sun's rays by a very complicated method—a strange scientific way called the Corioles force which has to do with the deflection caused by the rotation of the earth. Day-flying birds, too, lose their way if the sun is blotted out by clouds.

Nature automatically signals birds when it is time

to migrate. And when the urge comes, birds ignore everything else, often deserting their babies in the nest. They will fly for days until exhausted, covering vast distances and stopping only for occasional rests and any food they may be able to find on the way.

Birds are not the only ones who migrate. Many species of fish travel from one part of the ocean to another—eels, salmon and others. Some animals on land and even one species of worm are known to migrate.

Far up in the Arctic is the vast tundra—the treeless plains and stretches of marshy land covering hundreds of square miles. On the tundra are thick swarms of mosquitoes which provide food for baby birds. As the millions of birds arrive to spend the summer on their seasonal migration, there is a terrific noise with all their quacking, chirping and honking as they look forward to the plentiful feast of mosquitoes and other insects. All the birds are tired from the long flight but finally they get to the business of building their nests.

Migrating birds make some parts of the bleak Arctic look like a big, bustling city during the short summer months. There is jostling and crowding for nesting space, fights, food hunting and over all this, the young birds are trying out their wings with aerial acrobatics. They are preparing for the long fall flight to another part of the world.

There is one migrating bird, the arctic tern, that

flies eleven thousand miles just to lay two eggs and raise her chicks. This is a fantastic flight—all the way from the southern tip of South America, where the arctic tern spends its winters, to the Arctic, which is its summer home. This bird is the record long-distance flier of all the birds in the world and in order to cover this distance twice a year, in the spring and in the fall, it must spend months traveling.

Another bird that migrates to the Arctic is the golden plover. It spends its winters in the southern hemisphere and on its long journey does not eat one bit of food nor does it rest at all.

Other birds migrate to parts of the world nowhere near the Arctic. The ruby-throated hummingbird, smallest of all birds and about the size of a bumblebee, migrates every year from the northeast part of the United States to its winter feeding grounds in South America, a distance of about three thousand miles. How would you like to travel so far in order to find a good meal?

European warblers migrate all the way to Africa. And some of the long-necked, awkward-looking pink-feathered flamingoes travel to the marshes of Bonaire, an island in the West Indies, where they lay their eggs in a most unusual and funny-looking manner. They pile up mud into a cone-shaped small hill and on top of this mud, in a hollowed-out place, they lay their eggs.

74

The nests of the flamingos. The nests are made of mud and one egg is laid on the top of each.

STRANGE ANIMALS

If you will keep your eyes open you may be rewarded by seeing some strange sights when birds migrate, even though most of them travel too high in the air for you to watch them without binoculars. However, you might happen to look up into the sky one day and see a large flock of migrating geese or ducks flying in V formation. Don't feel as if the bird at the front of the V is to be envied because it is a leader, for actually, its job is extremely tiring and difficult. It is "splitting open the air" for the birds that are following it in the rest of the V formation. And because this first bird "splits" the air, the other birds are able to "slip" through the air more easily and follow in the cleared path the first bird has made for them. It is something like blazing a trail through the underbrush on land. That is why the bird at the head of the V formation gets tired quickly and must be replaced by one of the others very often.

Should you happen to see a migrating flock of herons or other big birds and then hear the chirping sounds of tiny birds, *don't* look for the small birds, for they are hiding. Where? In the feathers on the back of the larger birds. They are hitchhiking their way across oceans and mountains, taking advantage of the strong wings of the large birds and saving their own strength. Did I hear someone say that birds are dumb?

76

CHAPTER 13

Sneak Thieves

It would be awful if some night you awakened to see an ugly little black flying animal with pointed, furry ears and a gaping mouth out of which projected needle-sharp teeth. If this ever did happen you would know that you were face to face with a vampire bat—an animal that has a horrible habit. It steals blood!

Of course, you would never see this creature unless you lived where vampire bats are found, in Central or South America, and perhaps only if you were sleeping out in the open or had no screens on your windows.

If a vampire bat did attack you, the chances are you would never even awaken, for these vicious animals are able to puncture tiny holes in the skins of their

Vampire bat

victims, skillfully and painlessly. Then they lap up the blood as it oozes to the surface. Vampires strike at night. Usually the victims are livestock, wild animals or large seabirds, but they have been known to steal blood from humans, too.

The vampire bat is the only animal known that lives entirely on blood. Often these creatures drink so much blood that they leave their victim weak, and themselves become too heavy to fly. What a ghastly way to get dinner! It makes you shudder to think about it. It's lucky for us that bats in North America are not vampires but are harmless ones that eat only insects.

Bats are the only flying mammals in the world and the vampire is the only dangerous species. All bats, when they sleep, have a strange habit of hanging upside down in caves, under cliffs or in the hollows of tree trunks. They have very poor eyesight, but the sounds they emit, although too high pitched for us to hear, enable them to find their way as they fly in the dark. Their own squeaky sounds echo back to them like a radar beam, indicating direction and distance. In this way they are able to avoid obstacles in the blackness of their caves and to grab insects for food when they do their nightly foraging. The idea of our own radar systems, which help ships and planes in navigating, first came from bats.

79

We should be thankful that we did not live in the Age of Reptiles for, at that time, there lived a gigantic, winged lizard, the *pterodactyl*. Some of these flying monsters had a wingspread of almost thirty feet. If these creatures had been blood thieves we would, indeed, have been in a fix.

You may never have to worry about being attacked by a vampire bat but there *is* a tiny blood-sucking animal that has probably bitten you many times. Have you guessed what this sneak thief is? Yes, a mosquito! And it is the female that sucks blood; the male lives on plant juices. Of course a mosquito gets only a tiny bit of blood compared to the vampire bat, but all mosquitoes should be destroyed, for certain ones spread such diseases as malaria and yellow fever.

The female mosquito has a unique way in which she lays her several hundred eggs in order to be sure they hatch. She lays them on still waters so that they form a tiny raft. In a few days the eggs hatch into "wrigglers." These baby insects hang head down and each has a breathing tube that sticks up above the water. The wriggler then changes to a pupa and in a few days a full-grown mosquito emerges, flies away, and lives in the air, only returning to water when it deposits its eggs.

Among other parasite blood thieves that live on

their hosts are certain kinds of ticks, lice, and fleas. All should be killed for they are disease carriers. Sometimes the most deadly are the tiny or even microscopic ones. But none of them seems to fill people with such terror as the ugly vampire bat.

CHAPTER 14

Ocean Animal Wonders

Some places in our oceans have rocklike coral reefs which might be called underwater apartment houses. Many different kinds of fishes live permanently in the holes and niches of these reefs. These fish are stay-at-homes, spending all their lives in the coral reefs—or until such time as they might land either inside a frying pan or the stomach of another fish. There are still other fishes that are like gypsies, wandering through hundreds of miles of water, going where the food supply is best. The least known of all creatures of our oceans are the deep-sea fishes that live in the cold, black, unknown depths. Some of these are a complete mystery, yet we do know about a few and they are the most unusual creatures in the salty oceans.

82

Let us take a dive into the deep sea and have a look at some of them. We cannot use an aqualung outfit or a deep-sea diving suit, for this kind of equipment is only for comparatively shallow water. If we are to go down to where the queer deep-sea creatures are—down where it is as black as night, where the pressure is terrific and the water ice cold—we must use a metal container called a bathyscaphe. August Piccard invented the bathyscaphe *Trieste* which descended to an amazing depth. For the first time in the history of the world, the ocean bottom was studied at a depth of over two and a half miles.

Many deep-sea fishes are luminescent. This means they light up brightly like a lantern or electric light bulb, glowing like hot coals in the black ocean. They do this at will, with a certain substance they are able to manufacture. It is believed these fishes light up either to attract their own kind, to frighten off enemies, to attract prey, or in order to see better in the darkness. Isn't this similar to the fireflies on land calling their mates in the black of night with luminescent flashes of their body?

In the mysterious deeps there is one fish that has its lighting organs dangling from beneath its jaw. Another has its lighting organs arranged along the side of its body. There are some fish with jaws full of sharp spikelike teeth, looking like fearful monsters. There is also a "fisherman" fish below. This is the

Deep-sea angler fish

deep-sea angler. A sort of fishing rod is attached to the head of the female and the very tip of this rod glows like a small light on a Christmas tree. This light attracts other fish and when they come to investigate, the angler fish snaps them up for dinner.

A deep-sea fish named birkenia is an odd one. In spite of its big name this is a tiny fish, measuring eight inches. Birkenia is known to have lived as far back as three hundred and forty million years ago. The strange part about this fish is that it has no jaws. How does it eat without jaws, you will ask. By gulping its food whole, of course!

The eyes of deep-sea fishes are different from the eyes of other fishes; they may be enlarged or protruding. Some deep-sea fishes are entirely blind and they use their feelers or long fins in place of eyes in order to find food or to sense danger.

There are even greedy gluttons in the sea basement. One fish named *Chiasmodon* swallows other fish three times as big as itself. Down the fish goes, almost choking *Chiasmodon*, whose stomach stretches like a flexible rubber band, distending so much that it looks as if it would burst. In order for you to picture this, try imagining a mouse swallowing an elephant whole.

The next time you eat too much turkey on Thanksgiving and you feel as if you are going to pop, just think of the *Chiasmodon*.

CHAPTER 15

Honey Hunt

When you eat honey, nicely bottled or perhaps right from the comb made by the honeybees, you know that somewhere men have collected it from beehives in order to provide you with sweets. But in many other places of the world honey is not always delivered right to the grocery store. Often there are "honey hunters" and it might require long hours in the woods in order to find a beehive full of honey. Sometimes the honey hunters are men; sometimes animals hunt honey for themselves. In Africa, India, and South America, certain natives find their honey in a funny way with the help of a bird called an indicator major or "honey guide."

If you were one of these natives and suddenly

Indicator major (honey guide)

heard the churring sound of an indicator major re-peated over and over again, you would most likely stop whatever you were doing and follow the bird that was fluttering on ahead, leading the way and giving its "honey call." And you would probably have company. There might be a baboon following the call of this honey-guide bird or there might be a small, badgerlike animal called a ratel. A ratel looks very much like a skunk and loves to eat honey.

The ratel would follow the honey-guide bird quickly, arriving at the beehive first. Or if a larger animal got there at the same time, the ratel would put up a good fight with its sharp claws and teeth in order to protect its new-found meal of honey. Not many animals will attack a ratel for it is known to be an excellent and vicious fighter.

With several animals following the chirruping of the indicator major it might be best for you to hide behind a bush and watch the unusual proceedings that take place, instead of trying to get at the honey yourself.

After the honey guide is satisfied that the ratel has found the beehive, it perches quietly on the limb of a tree and waits. Then the ratel tears into the hive and pulls out the honeycombs. The angry bees buzz and sting, but the ratel's thick coat of fur protects it. After the ratel pulls out the combs it eats the honey.

88

Ratel

This animal is a real glutton and never gets enough.

It seems that the indicator major has been doing this kind of honey hunting, with the help of a ratel or sometimes a baboon or man, for centuries. The bird knows that, with its short beak, it will be unable to tear the honeycomb from its hiding place. And it also knows that its brown feathers, tinged with yellow, are no protection against the stings of a swarm of angry bees. So it has figured out a way to get help by leading others to the hive. Both animals and man know that the chirruping sounds of the honey guide mean, "Follow me, I've found some honey."

The indicator major does not care if it leads a ratel, a baboon or a man to the hive, just as long as it attracts someone who will find the hive and tear it out of the tree where the bees have hidden it.

By this time you are probably thinking that the honey-guide bird is awfully stupid. Why lead an animal to a beehive full of honey if the animal eats all the honey? Why doesn't the indicator major figure out some way to keep all the honey for itself after it goes to the trouble of finding the hive?

The answer to this is a most unusual one. The honey-guide bird does *not* like honey. It eats only the beeswax. And in order to eat the beeswax it must get someone to pry the combs from where the bees have stored them. When an animal or man tears up a hive, there is certain to be honeycomb strewn about, and the indicator major feasts on this wax.

Whether man or beast happens to get to the honey, the finder is extremely satisfied. The indicator is satisfied in getting the beeswax. So everyone is happy with this odd symbiotic arrangement; that is, everyone except the bees.

CHAPTER 16

Runaways from Home

Do you know about the odd behavior of the small, mouselike animals called lemmings? Here is a mystery which is one of the most baffling of the animal world.

Every few years these animals, which are about five inches long and look like rodents, leave their underground homes in the far north. Thousands of them take off on a long journey across the tundra. No lemming ever returns to the place where it lived. And only a few that start out on this journey remain alive. This is a death march!

The lemming is very well equipped for Arctic living where temperatures often drop to eighty degrees below zero. It has a tiny tail, a thick coat of fluffy, golden brown fur, and the bottoms of its feet are heavily padded with fur. Even its short ears are buried in this fine, silky hair.

Nature gave a helping hand, in a very practical way, to the little lemming, whose whole life depends upon how well it is able to dig. In the fall, an extremely long claw or "digging toe" grows on each foot. This is located under its normal claws. In the spring these long claws are shed. During the winter these "toe-diggers" help the lemming to dig out the tangled stems, roots and moss it uses for food, and also to dig deep under the snow and into the ground for its tunnel homes.

For years at a time lemmings seem to be quite content in the mazes of crisscrossed underground runways where they live in large colonies. The females have as many as five litters of young each year and they must keep on digging in order to enlarge their tunnel cities as their population increases. After a few years their underground apartments become crowded. All of the roots and moss have been eaten and the feeding grounds are barren. The tiny animals are desperate for food.

Suddenly the lemmings have an overpowering urge to get out of their tunnel cities. All of them at the same time decide to run away from home. They frantically dig out of their maze of tunnels and out of the snow until thousands of squealing lemmings

Lemming

are swarming over the tundra. On their short little legs they scurry *away* from their tunnel cities as fast as they are able to go. Usually they travel in rows three feet apart, just like marching soldiers, only the lemmings spread out in a fanlike formation.

As they rush on they are joined by the populations of other lemming cities until there are tens of thousands on the move. They pay no attention to any obstacle in their path. They swim deep rivers; some are drowned. When they come to a cliff they tumble over; some are killed. They march across valleys and scale high rocks. If you were in their way they would most likely climb all over you and keep on going. Once they start on their death march neither fire nor water stops them, nor even the savage foxes, wolves, bears, owls, weasels and other Arctic animals that slaughter and eat thousands of them. Often their march lasts for a year or more. The mass emigration covers hundreds of miles and they stop only to eat and rest.

Finally, a great many lemmings reach the sea. They plunge into the water and deliberately swim away from shore. Perhaps they think they are just crossing another narrow river. As they get farther away from land the lemmings become exhausted and die. Soon the ocean becomes a bloody mass of tiny, furred lemming bodies as the fishes and birds have a feast.

95

It is lucky that the entire lemming population of the world does not join in these strange death marches and all head for the sea, for if they did, there would have been no lemmings left on our planet many years ago. But there are always some that do *not* end up in the ocean. These remain alive to start new lemming cities.

The mass emigration of lemmings is fantastic. What if, suddenly, in your own town or city all the people left their homes and started on a journey that ended in certain death to a great many of them? Comfortable homes would be empty. The city would be desolate and deserted. Everyone would march and march many weary miles, going as fast as he could. It would be silly to leave your home, wouldn't it, unless you had a very good reason? Then *why* do lemmings leave *their* homes? If it is for lack of food, then why don't they travel a few miles and stop when they come to good feeding grounds? Why do they keep on going and going to mass destruction for so many of them?

Another mystery, equally puzzling in the animal world, concerns the huge twenty-eight-foot-long blackfish. These fish, members of the dolphin family, often behave in just as silly a way as the lemmings.

From the coast of Cape Cod and all the way to the Florida coast, groups of blackfish sometimes swim *out* of the deep Atlantic waters and head for shallow water. They deliberately leave their deep-water homes and swim right to shore. Men in boats have tried, with ropes, to lead or haul these enormous fish back into deep water again. But it is no use. They turn right around and swim to the shallow waters of shore again. Without sufficient water to support their immense weight, they soon die. Their carcasses must be towed by boats far out to sea.

Some say that blackfish are afraid to swim back into the deep water because they have enemies waiting out there for them. Those vicious predators of the sea, killer whales, who hunt in packs like wolves, are the natural enemies of blackfish. Perhaps it is these killer whales who drive the blackfish ashore.

The mystery of lemmings and blackfish has not, as yet, been solved. What do *you* think are the real reasons for the lemming death march and the mass suicide of blackfish?

CHAPTER 17

Odd Arctic Animals

Don't ever grab a polar bear's tail just to see what happens, for it would probably claw you to death. A polar bear permits only its own cub to do that. A young bear will often grab its mother's tail and hold on with sharp baby teeth while she swims ahead, pulling her cub through the water and out of danger.

The Arctic region right at the top of the world is where a baby bear often gets this kind of free tail ride. And there are other happenings, just as unusual, which take place in this frigid zone.

The Arctic is one of the least known areas of the world. Explorers have penetrated many miles into this white wilderness of snow drifts and ice, but it is still, in many respects, an area of great mystery.

Polar bear and cubs

You would think that the Arctic is so cold and bleak that no animal could survive there the whole year around. But this is not true. There are some animals that live in the cold and snow all the time and love it. In fact, they would be uncomfortable in a tropical country with their heavy coats of fur and their thick layers of fat beneath this fur. Perhaps they even think *we* are foolish to leave the cold climates at winter time, as so many of us do, and seek out warm areas in the south.

When some of the deep snow melts during the short Arctic summer, the frozen tundra becomes green and spongy underfoot from all the melting water. And it is in this vast tundra that mosses and lichens grow. These are food for many of the permanent animal dwellers of the north as well as for some of the migrating birds that come to the Arctic from all parts of the world.

Two of the most interesting of these cold-loving animals are the polar bear and the ringed seal. They both have thick fur and heavy fat layers to help keep them warm, but it still makes one shiver just to think of their being in temperatures that often drop to eighty degrees below zero, staying in this freezing cold throughout the long Arctic winter.

A full-grown polar bear may weigh as much as fifteen hundred pounds. Its fur is white and blends with the surrounding snow. With the help of this white camouflage a polar bear is able to creep up and surprise an animal it is stalking for food. The only time a polar bear gets into any kind of a shelter is when the female is about to give birth to its one or two cubs. She travels away from the water's edge and goes inland, over the ice and snow for as far as forty miles. Then she digs a "den" in a snowdrift, curls up and goes to sleep.

You would never be able to find a polar bear's den for, as the snow falls, it covers up the entrance completely. No one would guess that inside the den it is nice and warm from the body heat of the female. And it is a good thing the den is warm, for the cubs, when born in January, are almost hairless and weigh only around two pounds. Their eyes remain closed for six weeks after birth and they are completely helpless. It is hard to believe that in about a year they will each weigh around two hundred pounds. The polar bear is a good mother and keeps her cubs with her a whole year before they go into the wilderness of the Arctic to forage for themselves.

In the spring when the cubs have a coat of downy fur, they come out of the den with their mother. Then the fun begins for the baby bears. They have make-believe fights in the snow with each other and are taught by their mother how to find roots and

101

Ringed seal

plants. Then, as they get a little older, they learn how to catch mice and other tiny animals for food. Finally, the cubs begin to learn how to overtake their main source of food, the ringed seal.

A polar bear is an excellent swimmer but not fast enough to catch a seal in the water, so it must stalk the seal when this animal comes up on the ice. The bear creeps up to a seal, flattening its body on the ice and moves very slowly and quietly so as not to be seen or heard. And here is an unusual part about this hunt for food. The polar bear knows that the sleeping seal will raise its head and look around for any sign of danger *every seven seconds,* then will go back to sleep. The bear has figured out this timing perfectly. It becomes still just before the seal raises its head to look around. Then, when the seal is again taking its catnap, the bear creeps up closer. Often it takes a polar bear several hours to stalk a seal, but when it has finally gotten close enough, it gives a quick leap, killing the seal instantly. The seal is not fast enough to scurry for one of its air holes in the ice and dive into the water.

After all this work in stalking you would think that the polar bear would enjoy the fresh meat. But it does not even eat it. The bear devours only the thick layers of seal fat, leaving the meat for birds and other animals to feast upon.

You probably think that the polar bear is cruel eating the cute ringed seal, but with all wild animals, survival is the most important thing. Remember, they have no grocery store or milkman, so they must forage for themselves.

Are you wondering what kind of life the ringed seal leads if it is always stalked by polar bears? Well, they have a rough time of it and do not lead an easy life.

First of all, you should know that the ringed seal ranges farther north than any other mammal on our planet. It is called a ringed seal because its coat is marked with white rings that have dark centers. The animal spends most of its time beneath the ice fishing for shrimp, flounder and other Arctic sea food. It always swallows a fish head first so that its throat will not be hurt by the fins and scales. Being a mammal, the seal must breathe air and usually stays beneath the surface of the water for eight minutes at a time, but it can go without air for as long as twenty minutes at one time. And that is where it has troubles and problems.

Before the ringed seal goes fishing in the cold Arctic waters, it makes several air holes for itself by gnawing through the thick ice. Sometimes the fishing below is not so good and the seal must hunt farther away from the air holes than it should, or

104

often these holes freeze over. So when it is time to fill its lungs with air, the animal must quickly find one of its air holes. Sometimes the seal becomes desperate when it cannot find one. You try staying below water, holding your breath until your lungs cry out for air, then you will know just what this animal goes through as it hunts for an air hole.

The ringed seal has still another serious problem in its fight to keep alive. Sometimes during a storm it gets caught on the ice and it cannot find an air hole, or the ice is too thick to gnaw an air hole through. Then the seal stands the chance of starving to death, for it is cut off from its diet of fish and shrimp. Besides, the seal cannot protect itself by diving into an air hole, so it becomes easy prey for a polar bear.

You can see that the life of a ringed seal is full of danger. If they lived in herds, as do some other species of seals, they would have an easier time. But both the ringed seal and polar bear are "loners." They do their hunting and living, each in its own way, but entirely alone and dependent upon only themselves.

How lucky are the domestic animals that live in warmth and comfort, unlike the polar bear and ringed seal that dwell in the freezing Arctic, surrounded by all kinds of dangers.

CHAPTER 18

Three-Eyed Monsters

Imagine yourself paddling along in a canoe on a lonely river in prehistoric times—back millions of years when only animals inhabited the earth. Up ahead on the marshy bank you notice some kind of huge animal and your heart beats wildly. What can it be? Is it dangerous?

As you come closer you see that it is a giant frog-like monster over eight feet long. It squats in the mud, half hidden behind some tropical ferns, glaring at you. In alarmed surprise you stop the canoe, for what you see is fantastic! This creature has *three eyes.* The third eye is in the middle of its forehead.

The monster opens its enormous mouth which is full of long, sharp teeth. Then it lets out a frightening, froglike croak.

Eryops

By this time you have headed the canoe away from prehistory and are hurrying back into our modern age.

This extinct, prehistoric monster is *Eryops*, an animal which can put terror into the bravest person on earth. *Eryops* was an amphibian—an animal which can live on land or in water just as our frogs of today do. Amphibians lay jelly-covered eggs on the water, which later hatch into larvae or tadpoles. These water-living tadpoles breathe by means of gills, but when

107

adulthood is reached, amphibians become lung-breathing, land-living animals.

No one knows everything about the life cycle of *Eryops*, as at that time there were no humans, so there was no one to study this odd amphibian. But scientists do know that *Eryops* had a mouth as big as a hippopotamus', which looked like a cross between an alligator's and frog's mouth. It had thick legs which were so short that its stomach dragged along close to the ground when it walked. But the most remarkable thing about *Eryops* was that it was the first animal with a *voice*. Up until this time in history, no animal on earth had ever made a sound. Not a squeak or roar or a croak was heard on our planet until ugly *Eryops* was born.

Now, do you want to head that canoe back again into prehistory and try to capture a dangerous *Eryops*? Maybe, instead, it would be less hazardous and more fun to hunt for an animal with three eyes that is living today in our own times. It is a relative of one of the most ancient animals that lived on earth millions of years ago. This modern three-eyed monster is a tuatara, descendant of prehistoric reptiles. You will have to go to faraway Stephens Island just off the New Zealand coast to do your hunting, for this is the only place where this creature lives.

The tuatara looks like a big two-foot-long gray

AMERICAN MUSEUM OF NATURAL HISTORY

Tuatara

lizard with hornlike spines on its head. Its feet are froglike, similar to the feet of an alligator. But a tuatara belongs to a group of reptiles all by itself; it is *not* a crocodile, alligator or lizard.

The third eye of the tuatara is set grotesquely on top of its head. Although this extra eye looks like a real honest-to-goodness eye, with a retina and lens, scientists are not sure whether or not the tuatara is really able to see with it.

No one is allowed to land on Stephens Island where tuataras live, for they are protected by law. But if you did go to the island you would get the surprise of your life at the strange way the tuatara lives. It shares a burrow in the ground with an ocean bird called a sooty shearwater. This bird is related to the petrel and albatross. Each burrow is about three feet long, except at the end where it widens into a room lined with grass and leaves.

The tuatara hunts for its food at night and the bird feeds during the day, so they do not get in each other's way too much. But at nesting time when the bird incubates her eggs, and even when the baby birds hatch out, the tuatara sleeps right alongside the bird family.

Usually reptiles eat birds' eggs and baby birds, but these two have arranged their lives so that they live together peaceably in this very strange way. It is believed by some scientists that the tuatara pays the sooty shearwater for the use of its burrow by keeping it clean and eating the centipedes and other insects that invade the nest.

CHAPTER 19

Nature's Tricks

If you tried to look behind you without turning your head or if you wanted to look up at the exact second you looked down, it would be impossible. Yet there is a little black insect called a whirligig beetle that not only is able to see in all directions at the same time but is remarkable in other ways, too.

Swimming or whirling on the surface of a pond, this beetle can dive down into the water if a bird goes after it, or, if a hungry fish appears beneath it, off it flies. Most insects dwell either on land or in water but the whirligig beetle is able to do both. Actually, this insect has two sets of eyes. As it swims on the surface of the water one set of eyes is above the water and the other set is below the water. Of course, it has compound eyes as do most insects.

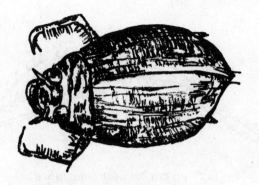

Whirligig beetle

The whirligig beetle has another very neat trick. When it wants to dive into the water it carries a bubble of air down with it at the tip of its abdomen. In this way, it carries its own oxygen bubble so that it may breathe under water. This is somewhat like an aqualung diver who carries his own air in a metal tube on his back, breathing in the air of this metal tube through a face mask.

Eggs of whirligig beetles are laid on water plants, and when they hatch into larvae they are known as water tigers, probably because they attack small fish, water insects and even one another. In about a month the larvae change into pupae and then, while turning into adults, they stay on the ground.

Whirligig beetles are easy to keep in an aquarium if you feed them tiny pieces of meat. It's fun to watch them carry their own oxygen bubbles when they dive.

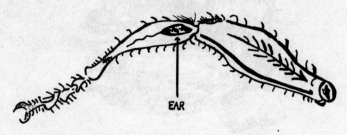

"Ear" on cricket's leg (magnified)

Nature often plays tricks, not only with insect eyes that contain many eyes but in misplacing ears, too! How would you like to have an ear on your leg instead of on your head? This is exactly where an insect called a katydid has its "ears"—on the upper part of its front legs.

Most katydids are green, with thin, leaflike wings that help to camouflage them as they feed on leaves of trees. However, there are some species that are pink or brown. The male is able to make the katydid "song" by rubbing the rasps and ridges located on the wing covers. This is similar to rubbing a bow on a fiddle. Perhaps with a little training they could produce the beautiful music of a violin instead of their monotonous katydid call.

114

Field crickets have ears located on their forelegs, too, and their shrill chirping at night is made by rubbing their forewings. The night noises of katydids and crickets are for the purpose of locating their own kind. It is not much different from when you know your mother is somewhere near and looking for you and you call out, "Here I am, mother."

Field cricket

CHAPTER 20

Living Fossils

Most of the animals that roamed over our earth millions of years ago have long been extinct. The only trace left of them is in fossils—skeletons of animals from million of years past that are found in rock layers of sandstone, slate or limestone. Most of the prehistoric fossils have been discovered by scientists and amateur fossil hunters. However, a few of these prehistoric animals have descendants that are living today. The descendants are called "living fossils" and because of them, we are able to see, first hand, how some of their ancient relatives looked.

Suppose we go on an expedition to the island of Komodo in the Malay Archipelago where one of these grotesque living fossils is found. But if you scare

116

Komodo lizard

easily you had better stay home, for this animal, a prehistoric monster, is the Komodo "dragon."

The island of Komodo is volcanic, made up of jagged, black lava and huge boulders that were thrown out of the earth by some long-past volcano. There are a few grassy spots on the island and some native palm trees, but it is a bleak, semiarid place and certainly not where you would want to live. Let us proceed cautiously, for this animal is over five feet long and stronger than a bull.

We move carefully over the sharp lava, trying to find cover and keep hidden in the sparse foliage. Then, suddenly, we see the Komodo dragon. We are looking at an animal from the past, a prehistoric terror, almost unchanged from when it lived sixty million years ago. We drop close to the ground and watch.

The evil-looking beast moves slowly, slithering and scraping its ugly body over the lava. It has an enormous head, and jaws that are immense. As it opens its mouth we see long, sharp, spikelike teeth and a forked tongue which darts in and out between these teeth. Its tough hide is wrinkled and black, its legs are bent and close to the ground, and its feet have long claws. This animal is classed by scientists as the largest of all living-fossil lizards, the adults weighing about three hundred pounds. Even though they call it a lizard, it looks like a dragon to us.

118

The Komodo lizard turns to where we are in hiding. Will it find us? It lumbers dangerously near. Shall we run or stay hidden? There have been some Komodo lizards captured on other expeditions and taken to zoos or to museums to be stuffed and mounted, but we are just looking and not gathering specimens. We have no guns with us, no means of defense.

Finally the huge monster changes its mind and turns away from where we are in hiding. We are able to leave, unseen, and we make a hasty exit.

The three-eyed tuatara on the island of New Zealand is still another "living fossil." This large gray lizard also looks like its ancient relatives millions of years back in history, only it is much smaller than the Komodo dragon.

You do not have to go to faraway Komodo island or to New Zealand to find a living fossil. If you keep your eyes open you may find one right in your own yard—a dragonfly. Yes, the common dragonfly of today is related to a prehistoric insect genus, the *Meganeura*, a giant dragonfly that lived two hundred and fifteen million years ago. *Meganeura* were the largest known insects in the world. They had wingspreads of two feet across.

The modern dragonfly that lives today has silver-colored, gauzy, iridescent wings. It is about eight inches long, with a slender body, which is the reason

Dragonfly

it is often called "Devil's darning needle." But in spite of its nickname it does not sting.

The female dragonfly lays her eggs in the water of a pond or stream, sometimes fastening them to a plant. When the eggs hatch, their own mother probably does not even recognize them, for they do not look at all like dragonflies. The dragonfly nymph grows slowly, remaining in the water for two or three years. And, by a strange twist of nature, all the time the nymph remains in the water its lower intestine takes oxygen out of the water, acting as a gill. After its years in water the dragonfly nymph comes above the surface, sheds its skin and flies away on its beautiful silvery wings.

The dragonfly has very remarkable compound eyes. Each eye is made up of about thirty thousand tiny eyes. It is true that other insects have compound eyes, too, but none has as many tiny eyes as this insect.

A long, pointed lower lip is another remarkable thing about the dragonfly of today. As it hides in the grass and reeds it sticks this lip out quickly and gathers up food that floats by. Unfortunately, the interesting dragonfly has a very short life. It lives only from a few days to a year, depending upon the species.

It is lucky for us that the giant *Meganeura*, ancient relative of the present-day dragonfly, is extinct, for with a lower lip that perhaps functioned in the same way as does that of the modern dragonfly, it could be very dangerous. Imagine an enormous lip darting out, perhaps as far as two feet, quickly gathering in anything that looked like an appetizing meal. The *Meganeura* might even have developed into a "people eater" if people had been on the earth at that time. But this is highly improbable, for scientists know that the *Meganeura* had plenty to eat sixty million years ago. In those prehistoric times there were huge cockroaches swarming over our planet, so perhaps the giant dragonflies feasted on giant cockroaches and they would have had no interest in people, anyway.

CHAPTER 21

Odd Australian Mammals

Anyone who lives in Australia and likes teddy bears is lucky, for they have real live ones living in the woods here. These "teddy bears" are cute, thickly furred koala bears. They have noses that look like big black buttons, sleepy little eyes, large furry ears and stub tails. After you take a look at one of them, I'm sure you will agree that teddy bears are patterned after koala bears, which are really not bears at all. They are related to the opossum and are "marsupials" —animals that carry their young in a pouch. This pouch is usually loose folds of skin on the belly.

When born, the baby koala bear is about an inch long and it wriggles into its mother's pouch where it stays for several months. After the baby leaves the

Koala bears

pouch it rides on its mother's back, clinging onto her thick fur. And what an exciting time it has! For koala bears jump from tree to tree, often taking a flying leap as far as three feet. A baby koala bear must get a roller-coaster thrill ride each time its mother jumps.

The mother koala bear, about the size of a small dog, does not have too heavy a load to carry, for only one baby is born at a time. It is certainly fortunate she does not have as many as fifteen babies at one time like the opossum, another marsupial.

You will always find the koala bear of Australia in one particular place—where eucalyptus trees grow. There are many varieties of eucalyptus that flourish in Australia and these tall trees are both home and food to the cute koala bear. These mammals eat nothing else but the leaves of eucalyptus trees. And it is fun to watch them eat. They hold a branch in a front paw as they hold fast to the tree, then they slowly munch and chew the leaves. To a koala bear the eucalyptus leaves must taste like ice cream or candy does to us, for they certainly seem to enjoy them and never change their diet for anything else.

If you ever take a trip to Australia and do not get to go into the eucalyptus woods, you will be able to see koala bears at the zoo in Sydney. They might even let you hold one of them, but watch out for their sharp claws for they defend themselves against enemies

125

by means of their claws and their long jumps from tree to tree.

In Australia are found more marsupials than any other place in the world. In fact, two-thirds of Australia's mammals are marsupials. Among these are the Tasmanian devil, honey mouse, wombat, bandicoot, opossum, koala bear, and kangaroo. Australia also has birds found no other place in the world—emus, black swans, and kookaburras.

The reason for all the marsupials and strange birds living in Australia is that this continent has been separated from all the rest of the world, with an ocean surrounding it, for a very long time. This island-continent is almost halfway around the world from Europe, two thousand miles from the mainland of Asia and six thousand miles from the Americas. Because of this separation of Australia from other lands, animals from as far back as seventy-five million years ago had the chance to stay just as they were in primitive times, right up to our modern times. That is why many of the animals living in Australia today are "living fossils."

The koala bears are a lot better off than some of the other mammals of Australia. One group of marsupials, the kangaroos, has two enemies—the wild dog called dingo and the fox. Often a full-grown kangaroo, leaping fifteen to twenty feet at a time and

126

Kangaroo with baby in pouch

going at a speed of thirty miles an hour, will have a wild dog in hot pursuit. And, tucked in the fleeing kangaroo's pouch is her baby, or "joey," as it is called. A wild dog has a hard time catching up with a kangaroo, but while it is fleeing from the danger of a dingo, the kangaroo can meet its death in a very stupid way. Kangaroos have a habit of looking over their shoulders when traveling at high speed, and they are sometimes killed by smashing into a tree when running. They really get killed by not looking where they are going.

There are many kinds of kangaroos—tree-climbing ones, wallabys, and many others, and they all are like traveling gypsies, covering great distances and always moving from place to place. They must do this in order to keep alive, for they are herbivorous. They eat only plants and grasses, and the dry plains of Australia are sparsely covered with edible grazing grounds.

A full-grown kangaroo may weigh two hundred pounds and stand eight feet high. Their powerful hind legs and strong tails help carry them at breakneck speed, and they also use their tails and hind legs to defend themselves. On the kangaroo's big toe is a long, sharp, curved toenail that looks like a dagger and with their legs they are able to kill an animal with one powerful blow. Older kangaroos are short tempered, mean and dangerous, so everyone keeps safely away from them unless hunting them.

The ring-tailed rock wallaby, smallest member of the kangaroo family, is probably the cutest and most attractive of the kangaroo species. It is especially noted for its leaps, often over twelve feet in length, when it travels from boulder to boulder in the high places of Australia. The secret of the wallaby's success in these hazardous leaps is that its hind feet are padded and its soles are rough. As a wallaby jumps, these rough soles keep it from slipping. These small kangaroos can even climb a tree to get out of danger, clinging to the branches with middle toes that are capable of grasping and holding on tightly, just as a monkey's tail holds on tightly to a branch.

Baby kangaroos, like all marsupials, grope their way blindly into their mother's pouch right after they are born. Sometimes these newborn kangaroos cannot find the pouch and fall to the ground and die. You would never guess that a newborn kangaroo would some day grow larger than a man, for at birth it looks like a tiny, red grub. While the baby kangaroo lives in its mother's pouch for six months, it feeds on her milk. Then finally it sticks its head out, looks around at the world and leaves its mother's pouch. The joey begins to eat grass and leaves of young trees, which it bites off with its sharp lower teeth.

STRANGE ANIMALS

Almost every zoo you visit will have kangaroos. Next time you see one of them watch how the baby runs to its mother's pouch and gets in if it becomes frightened. Sometimes the baby kangaroo has grown too big to fit into the pouch. Then it will hide just its head in the pouch and it seems to feel sure no danger can get to it, even with its entire body in the open.

CHAPTER 22

"Pretend" Animals

It sounds unbelievable, but there are really "cleaners" among the fishes that swim in the sea just as we have laundries and dry cleaning establishments on land. There are about twenty species of cleaning fish —ranging from a tiny wrasse with stripes on its body to various other kinds. There are even a few shrimp, a worm and a crab that do cleaning also. These cleaners in the ocean do not put out signs saying, "Dry cleaning while you wait." Instead, they have a very odd way of getting customers.

The cleaner fish approaches a larger fish, often an enormous shark or ray, and begins to go through strange antics—darting back and forth, dancing around, flapping its tail up and down, and even nib-

Striped wrasse fish

bling on the body of the fish it wants to clean. This is the cleaner fish's way, in place of a sign, of saying, "I'm in the cleaning business. If you'll stop swimming for a few minutes and hold still, I'll take all those bothersome parasites off your body."

The larger fish never eats the small cleaner fish. Instead, it holds perfectly still while the cleaner gets to work, nibbling carefully with pointed teeth, going over the larger fish's whole body and ridding it of fungus growths and troublesome parasites. When the cleaner comes to a fin, it pokes the fish until the fin is raised, then it cleans under the fin, goes on to clean the gill coverings and even inside the larger fish's mouth.

Of course, the cleaner fish is not in business just for fun. It eats the bacteria, parasites and food particles, thus getting a full meal. Each fish is doing the other a favor; one gets rid of parasites, the other has a free dinner. This is a good example of symbiosis.

Often a fish wanting to be cleaned will do funny tricks to attract a cleaner fish, like standing on its head or rolling over on its side. The cleaner takes the hint and gets to work. Sometimes fish loaded with parasites will wait in line until their turn comes up for cleaning. And they even get into fights while they are waiting, for each one wants to be cleaned first.

Sometimes a fish villain steps into the picture and

does a very mean thing, taking unfair advantage of a fish that needs to be cleaned. This villain is a savage predator that lives in the Indian Ocean and has the fancy scientific name of *Aspindontus taeniatus*. It is blue with bars on its sides, looking just like some of the cleaner fish. It approaches a fish that needs the parasites taken off, flapping its tail and going through the antics which, in fish language, mean, "I'll do a cleaning job for you." But instead of cleaning the customer, the villain *Aspindontus taeniatus*, with its long, sharp teeth, will tear chunks out of the un- suspecting fish that was fooled into thinking it was a friendly cleaner.

The *Aspindontus taeniatus* has just practiced "mimicry," pretending to be something that it is not. If you think that humans are the only ones who pre- tend and imitate, you are mistaken, for animals do it, too. When people pretend, they do so because they are play acting or just for fun. But when animals pretend, they have a more serious purpose; they want to pro- tect themselves or they are trying to appear as some- thing that they are not in order to attract food.

Many animals practice mimicry. One is the viceroy butterfly, which would make a delicious meal for a bird, but it is never eaten because it looks so much like the bad-tasting monarch butterfly. There are flies that are perfectly harmless and unable to sting which look like stinging wasps. And there are still more fantastic ways that some animals use to imitate or practice mimicry.

Suppose you were a newborn fish just hatched somewhere around the Great Barrier Reef and you were being chased by a larger fish. What would *you* do? Hide, of course, for the predator fish would be much too big for you to fight. So you dash for the nearest place of safety, which would probably be an underwater rock or plant. You are terribly frightened and you press close to a flowerlike plant, glad to be under its thousands of protective petals. You hope the predator fish that is trying to make a meal of you will not be able to see where you are hiding.

Suddenly you are seized by one of the petals of the flower. Still another petal encircles you, squeezing and strangling. Then you realize you have made a terrible mistake! This is not a plant, this is an *animal* that *pretends* to be a beautifully colored flower in order to fool victims into its trap. What appears to be a harmless plant is really a fish-eating animal, a giant two-foot-wide sea anemone called a *Discosoma*.

The petals of the anemone are fleshy tentacles which surround its mouth. And its mouth is also its stomach. Once a tiny fish is caught by a sea anemone, there is no getting away. The tentacles do the grabbing and stinging cells kill the victim. The sea anem-

135

Sea anemone

one closes up like some land flowers do at night, and then the combination mouth-stomach digests the tiny fish. Some anemones are less than an inch wide, others are enormous, and all obtain their food by practicing mimicry.

The *Discosoma* has a partner in crime. This is the tiny, brilliantly colored clownfish which lives in the same waters as *Discosoma*—the Great Barrier Reef of Australia. The clownfish is bright orange with three white bands with black borders and this attractive fish has a most extraordinary home, right in the tentacles of the huge sea anemone. The clownfish swims in and out of the tentacles without ever getting hurt, but it plays a mean trick on other fish. It lures them into the death trap of the *Discosoma*. Then both the clownfish and giant anemone share this dinner. The clownfish also massages the tentacles of the *Discosoma*. No one knows why the giant anemone allows only the clownfish to roam in and out of its dangerous tentacles without any harm. This is one of the mysteries of the deep sea.

CHAPTER 23

Fair Exchange

Did you know that plants and animals are very important to each other in a way that neither is aware of? In fact, plants could not live without animals' breathing and animals could not live without plants' breathing.

You and all animals in the world breathe in oxygen, then breathe out and expel carbon dioxide. The plants need this carbon dioxide. They breathe it in through their leaves and, by a complicated chemical process called *photosynthesis*, they combine sunlight and water from the soil, manufacturing starch and sugar for their food. And while they manufacture food for their own use, plants give out oxygen and moisture into the air through the pores in their leaves.

A remarkable pigment of green-leaf foliage called chlorophyll helps in this magical process. It aids the plants to manufacture starch and sugar and to maintain the supply of oxygen in the air.

This exchange of air is just as necessary to animals as is food and is as important to plants as are soil and water.

In water this same kind of miracle exchange occurs, too. Oxygen rises toward the surface water from plants and leaves. Fish breathe in this oxygen. And the plants breathe in the carbon dioxide expelled by the fish. The plants also are supplied with their mineral requirements by the waste products of fishes.

If plants were suddenly to stop producing oxygen all humans and animals on earth would suffocate and die. And if there were no carbon dioxide produced by animals, the plants would dry up and die. If this were ever to happen, there would no longer be any life at all on our earth.

CHAPTER 24

Jumbos with Three Lips

When flying over a jungle in a plane you see a lovely green carpet, a vast sea of tree tops beneath you. But if you go on foot into this same jungle you find it is not like a carpet at all but is often a dense, wild tangle of impenetrable growth made up of thousands of acres of trees and plants. It takes seconds to fly over one mile of jungle whereas every mile you go on foot might take many weary days.

Suppose we go into one of the jungles in India, a wild, tropical, steaming place where odd creatures lurk in the shadows and matted growth. We are on an elephant hunt! Not with guns, but with words, for we are going to ask questions and find out all we can about this remarkable jumbo beast, largest land animal on earth.

We come to a village in the heart of an Indian

140

jungle and, through an interpreter, we ask the chief the age-old question, "Do elephants go to a secret place to die—a hidden valley where there are supposed to be tons of ivory tusks strewn about, along with the bones of these dead pachyderms?"

But no one can answer this question—neither the chief nor any of the Indians—for no human being has ever found a secret elephant burial ground, although for centuries there have been rumors of their existence. If anyone ever did find such a place it would be like discovering a gold mine, for the ivory tusks, weighing over one hundred pounds each, are very scarce and worth a great deal of money.

The natives of this village in India tell us many interesting things about elephants, for they capture and train these six-ton jumbos for zoos and circuses, to help in their own heavy tasks, and for hunting.

Usually two female elephants go along as nursemaids to a secluded spot with an elephant about to have an offspring. These nursemaids keep the others of the herd from bothering the weak, newborn infant. Elephants are exceptionally good mothers, but if baby gets out of line and needs to be punished, mama whacks baby with her trunk.

Do you know what the elephant's trunk is really used for, besides spanking baby? Most people think it is a large tube through which the elephant sucks water and food. But it is not. Really, the trunk is a remarkable invention of nature which enables the elephant to pick up food and stuff it into its mouth and to suck up water and squirt it down its throat. In addition, the trunk is used to sniff the air to scent an enemy, to break off branches of trees, and to test the ground in order to see if it is solid enough to walk on.

Actually, the trunk is made up of the upper lip and nose, giving jumbo *two* lips on the end of its trunk. The elephant also has a lower lip, which gives it a total of three lips in all. Just look at what *you* are able to do with your *two* lips; no wonder the elephant is extremely clever with its *three* lips.

It takes patience and time to train elephants, but they have greater intelligence than even horses. They are especially superior in the jungle work of stacking huge logs into neat piles. They are the only animals, outside of the primates—the highest order of mammals, to which human beings belong and also the apes, monkeys, and lemurs—that seem to understand the mechanical principle of a log slide. They maneuver the logs carefully into position with their trunks, then give this tall, heavy pile a quick push with their forefeet. They seem to enjoy watching as the logs roll into the water with a big splash. Later, of course, these logs are floated down the river by natives, then cut into boards.

In circuses and zoos you will most likely see ele-

phants from India, called Asiatic elephants, instead
of those from Africa. The reason for this is that Asiatic elephants are easier to capture and train while
the African species usually remains wild in captivity,
is easily frightened, and is very unpredictable in behavior.

An easy way to tell if an elephant is from India or
Africa is to look at its ears. The Asiatic elephant's
ears are small and sort of look like the map of India.
The African elephant's ears are so large and floppy
that they hang halfway to the ground.

In circuses, only the chimpanzees and orangutans
learn faster than elephants. Elephants learn many
stunts, among which are jumping rope, standing on
their heads, sitting on an upside-down tub, kneeling,
and lifting their feet to shake hands. Perhaps you
have been to a circus and seen how elephants march
in single file, each elephant holding on to the tail of
the elephant ahead. Sometimes an elephant becomes
unruly and the keeper cannot handle it. Then an
older elephant comes to the rescue. This oldster will
lash out with its trunk, spanking the unruly jumbo
until all is well again.

Most elephants eat one hundred and fifty pounds
of food and drink fifty gallons of water a day. They
would be quite expensive pets, wouldn't they? And
most are extremely curious and mischievous. One of

143

the most famous in captivity, called Coco, used always to pull a little dog's tail if it got the chance, and would also pull off the coat of any zoo attendant that came nearby. Once Coco tried to pull down the gas pipes that were in his cage, and another time he tried to eat an electric light globe, but it was taken away from him just in time. Coco almost flooded the circus grounds when he turned on a water faucet one dark night. He would always try to do this same trick, again and again. Another stunt Coco did was not so nice. He would trumpet wildly for no reason at all, and when one elephant roars all the others around come to its aid. They break the chains on their legs, mill around in all directions, and there is a real elephant stampede.

Modern elephants had relatives that lived in ancient times. These were three-lipped jumbos, too, which stood ten feet high, weighed even more than elephants do today, and had longer tusks. They were called mastodons and mammoths. At one time there were so many of these pachyderms that the ground must have trembled with their weight as they traveled to their feeding grounds, stamping and crashing through the trees in great herds.

In the north polar region, which in ancient times did not remain frozen all of the time as it does now, many of these mammoths met their death in an odd way.

Mammoth

Just picture a herd of plant-eating mammoths roaming over the frozen tundra to a place that looks like good feeding grounds. Green shoots and leaves of plants are just showing up with the spring thaw. There is wild trumpeting as the gigantic mammoths make a dash for the green food. Then crash! Most of the herd sinks into mud. The ground beneath them is no longer frozen solid but has thawed into a mushy bog. With piercing screams and straining wildly, the huge animals try to pull their enormous feet out of the swamp that holds them fast. They are trapped! They sink down deeper and deeper. Slowly they die, and when the ground suddenly freezes over again, they are preserved for thousands of years. Many of these mammoth fossils have been dug up in our modern times, along with their ancient ivory tusks.

Where are the mammoths and mastodons today, you might ask? Well, no one knows exactly what happened to them. They completely vanished from the face of our planet. Only fossilized bones, ivory tusks and their relatives, the elephants, remain to remind us that once they overran our globe.

CHAPTER 25

Strange Uses for Animals

Termites are tiny antlike animals that feed on wood. Some termites have built-in squirt guns—snouts through which they spray enemies with a sticky liquid that entangles the victim's legs and stupefies it. It would be an excellent idea if we could use these squirt guns to help humans; that is, if the termites could be trained to squirt poison on themselves. For termites work in large groups and are extremely destructive, doing millions of dollars worth of damage each year. They can eat the foundation of a house so that the whole structure tumbles down, and spraying wth poison insecticides is one of the most important ways to get rid of them.

Using the squirt gun of a termite is no more fan-

147

tastic than the unusual use to which some animals have already been put all over the world, by certain people. A few of these strange uses for animals are briefly described for you.

A certain spider in Australia produces a six-foot, large meshed web. This gigantic web is used by the natives. How? you might ask. As fishing nets, of course! These webs are extremely strong and elastic and will hold any good-sized fish that gets trapped in them.

Another way that animals help humans is with skunk oil. You have probably, at some time, smelled the odor of foul-smelling skunk oil, which may be detected as far as half a mile away. An artificial skunk odor, butyl mercaptan, is used to save the lives of men. It is put into the ventilating systems and sent down below the earth's surface to warn men working in mines. In seconds, the nasty odor spreads to all mine shafts and tunnels. The miners know what this warning means—fire! And they quickly leave the mine.

We have animals to thank for many substances used in our everyday lives. Food, hides and fur are, of course, supplied by farm and wild animals, but did you know that many by-products are also supplied by animals and insects? Gelatine, honey, lard, and suet are just a few. Medicines and extracts used in healing

are also provided by some animals; for example, adren-
alin, beeswax, cod liver oil, insulin, lanoline, pepsin,
thyroid gland extract, and pituitary extract. Bat
guano, the residue from the "guano bat," is used in
making gunpowder.

Even birds work for humans. In some European
countries certain birds, called chimney sweeps, are
used to clean out soot-filled chimneys. And there are
also birds used as postmen! These are the man-o'-war
or frigate birds of the South Seas. The first step in
preparing a frigate bird to be a postman is to capture
it when it is young, and then to feed and make a pet
of it. A perch is erected on the beach, and when the
full grown frigate bird is finally released, the natives
can count on these birds always to alight on the
perches, if they are near their island. In this way,
messages are passed from island to island. This is a
most unusual kind of postal service!

Here is one peculiar trick with an insect you might
try yourself. Some of the natives of the West Indies
capture lightning bugs and fasten them to their feet.
Then, when going through the jungle at night, the
native's path is lighted with the on-and-off lumin-
escence that the animals manufacture. Here are insects that help mankind!

Sharks are very valuable in helping man. Long ago,
war clubs, spears and swords were covered with the

sharp teeth of sharks. And today, the liver of the shark is used for its oil, the skin is made into leather products, and the rough-textured skin has also been used by carpenters. Can you guess how? As sandpaper!

Did you ever hear of a dead fish that goes to war to help win battles for humans? Well, there is a certain fish that South Sea island warriors use, the porcupine fish, which is covered with sharp spines. The body of this fish is able to distend like a balloon when it becomes angry, so, when there is a battle to be fought, the South Sea island warrior first captures a porcupine fish. Then the fish is teased until it distends, puffing up until it is much bigger than the warrior's head. The fish is killed, cleaned, and dried. Finally, it is worn as a helmet, and the porcupine fish's sharp spines protect the native's head.

Would you believe that camels have often been used as smugglers? Yes, they smuggle opium and hashish, drugs which are not supposed to be sold or used except on a doctor's prescription for illness. The camels are really innocent victims of a smuggler's ring, yet they are the actual smugglers and this is the way it happens.

The camel's owner will fill small containers with opium, then force these down the animal's throat. The container goes into the camel's first stomach,

150

and here it may stay for weeks, until the Arab arrives at his destination with the smuggled drugs. Then the camel is butchered and the drugs removed and sold, unless the authorities catch the men behind the smuggling ring and capture the beasts that have, unwillingly, helped the smugglers.

CHAPTER 26

Marvels of Nature

The next time you have a guessing game be sure to ask the question, "What animal is fur bearing, has a bill like a duck, lays eggs and nurses its young?" Most likely no one will know the answer, so you will be able to surprise everyone and explain that this queer animal is a platypus, often called a duckbill, and that it is one of the strangest warm-blooded animals in the world.

The platypus is found only in the rivers and streams of eastern Australia and in nearby Tasmania, where it lives both on land and in water. It has four legs with web feet similar to those of a duck and thick fur on its body like that of a beaver. It also has a wide, flat tail and its nostrils are near the end of its soft,

Duckbilled platypus

rubbery bill. Measuring from the tip of its bill to the tip of its tail, a platypus grows to about twenty inches in length and weighs only four pounds.

Everything about the platypus is most unusual. The babies of all other mammals, with the exception of one called a spiny anteater or *echidna*, are born alive from the mother's body, but the platypus babies come from eggs. The duckbill lays her two pigeon-sized, soft-shelled eggs, then incubates them in a most peculiar fashion—by curling up in a ball and holding the eggs against her body with her tail. You would think her tail would get awfully tired holding on to the eggs for seven to ten days until they hatch, but duckbills have probably been doing this ever since they first appeared on our earth, and, as yet, they have not found a better way to hatch their eggs.

When the eggs finally hatch, the mother platypus has a funny way of nursing her babies. She does not have regular teats, as most mammals do, but the milk exudes from pores in the milk glands on her abdomen, and the babies lap up this thick, cheesy fluid.

Most of the time a platypus stays under water, where it swims and dives very well. Only the tip of its bill sticks out above the surface. It feeds at night on the river bottom, eating worms, crayfishes, and water insects. Using its bill to catch its dinner under water, it keeps its eyes shut tightly, finding food by touch and smell. Then it comes up to the surface to chew and swallow its food. You would never guess what the duckbill likes to eat in captivity, in addition to the same diet it usually eats in its native habitat. A platypus loves to eat egg custard!

A duckbill is very clumsy on land. It folds the webbing on its feet *under* its feet and the claws are used to help it walk. If it is a male beware if you try to pick it up! The male duckbill is the only poisonous mammal in the world. This cute-looking animal will growl like an angry dog and use the poison defense spurs on each hind leg. It will not go out of its way to look for a fight, but protects itself by sticking you with these spurs, injecting a poison like snake venom.

Are you wondering in what kind of a place the platypus lives? Even this is peculiar. In a mud bank it builds a grass-lined nest with an underground water entrance. Throughout the day the duckbill sleeps in its nest, then during the night becomes active.

Although the platypus is called a duckbill, it is not a relative of ducks. It is, along with the spiny anteater, called a *monotreme*. The platypus and spiny anteater are the only two kinds of mammals in the world that lay eggs. Both of them are the only *monotremes* in existence. It is believed they inhabited the earth as far back as one hundred and fifty million years ago.

The echidna has several advantages over its relative,

the platypus. Also a native of Australia and Tasmania, the spiny anteater lives on land and, after the mother lays her eggs, she hatches them in a pouch on her stomach. This is much easier than holding on to the eggs with her tail as the mother platypus does. The spiny anteater, as its name implies, has quills like a porcupine. As soon as the babies in the pouch develop spines of their own and they begin to stick the mother echidna, out they go. If danger threatens, the echidna burrows quickly into the ground. All you can see is a mound of earth and if you happen to step on this you will get a good sticking with the exposed quills. Ants and other insects do not have a chance when a spiny anteater is around, for this mammal has a foot-long, sticky tongue coiled in its thin beak. It darts its tongue out so quickly that you can hardly see it being done.

Years ago when no one had even heard of a *monotreme* the scientists in England thought a good joke was being played on them. One of the early settlers from Australia sent in the skin of a duckbill. The scientists at first did not believe this to be a really, honest-to-goodness animal. They thought that someone had fastened the flat bill of some kind of bird to the skin of an animal. Were they surprised when they found that this peculiar animal, the duckbill, really did exist. You can just see the mad rush of expedi-

Echidna or *spiny anteater*

tions to Australia as the scientists set out to find a live platypus. And when they did find the platypus and also the spiny anteater they decided that both are related to reptiles and also to the earliest mammals. These two *monotremes* are living fossils.

This proves that there is always something new to be found out about animals. Perhaps, if you become an amateur or professional scientist, you also might discover other *monotremes* that are living today. A platypus might be in a river near your home, as yet undiscovered. A spiny anteater could even be in a park nearby. Don't think this is impossible. Stranger things than these have been found! Just a few short years ago a *coelacanth* was discovered. This is a prehistoric fish that was supposed to be extinct for sixty million years. But a fisherman off the coast of Africa gathered in his catch one day and found this bright blue fish with odd-shaped fins, tail, and scales in his net. It was five feet long and weighed one hundred and twenty-five pounds. When the fisherman took it to a museum the odd fish was found to be a prehistoric *coelacanth*. This fisherman had made one of the most remarkable scientific discoveries in the world!

CHAPTER 27

Bee Dancers and Bee Bakers

A great many of the people in almost every country of the world have some kind of native dance. There are dances to celebrate harvest time; fun dances when people are happy; devil-chasing dances among primitive native tribes; and the American Indians used to do a war dance before going into fierce battle. And you will hardly believe this, but there is even an insect that dances!

This dancing insect is none other than the honeybee, and its dance tells a story. Bees cannot talk to one another like we do, so they dance in order to give messages to other bees in the hive. The message they give is most important—where to locate flower nectar, the sweet juice found in flowers from which they

159

*Worker bees perform a strange dance in order to tell
other bees exactly where they have located nectar*

make honey, their only food. Without honey they
would die.

Professor Karl von Frisch of the University of
Munich studied the habits of bees for many years and
finally he solved the great mystery that had puzzled
man for centuries—how bees communicate with
one another. And imagine his surprise when he found
out that bees dance in order to communicate.

Remember, bees are extremely important to our
everyday life. As they sip the nectar from flowers they
pick up the tiny grains of pollen from the stamen of
the blossom; it sticks to their "pollen baskets," which
are really stiff hairs on their back legs. As the bee flies
from flower to flower, this pollen rubs off and is

160

spread to the pistil of the blossom—the pistil is the seed-bearing organ in the center of the flower. In this way blossoms are fertilized so that they are able to develop into fruit or flowers. Some farmers even rent beehives and place them in their orchards. Then the farmers are *sure* the bees will be there to help pollinate the blossoms of their fruit trees. If it were not for bees you would not be eating oranges, apples and many of the other kinds of fruit you like and if it were not for bees there would be no crops in our fields. So it is no wonder that Professor von Frisch and other scientists spent so much time trying to find out about these important insects.

The dance of the bees is a strange one. As soon as a honeybee has found blossoms with nectar it rushes back to the hive and, with the other bees watching attentively, it begins an odd dance. First it turns around and around in a circle, then goes to the right, then to the left with quick steps. Or sometimes the bee doing the dance stays in exactly the same spot for a whole minute. Or the whole dance may be reversed, because as the bee dances it is giving directions.

Soon the other bees of the hive excitedly join in the dance, following each movement and keeping their feelers close to the bee giving them the message. If you were to peek into the hive at this moment you

161

Worker honeybee

would wonder at the cleverness of the bees as they interpret the language of the "bee dance." Certain movements mean, "The nectar is in blossoms west by northwest." Other movements of the dance mean, "Go east, for there you will find the flowers with nectar." Other dance steps mean, "The nectar is a mile away." Complete directions are given by the first bee until finally all the workers of the hive take off and head in the direction where the blossoms are to be found. And they always go to the exact spot where the first bee found the nectar.

If you want to know what a bee gets when it sucks nectar, try pulling a flower and sucking the end of it.

You will taste a tiny droplet of sweet juice, which is the nectar the honeybees gather. A worker bee lives only six weeks but during its short life it spends all of its time gathering nectar from thousands of blossoms. It is not much fun to work all the time, but that is why they are called worker bees. And the odd part of the bees' social life is that the workers are always females that cannot have children.

Honeybees live in big groups, with around fifty thousand in a single hive. Their hive is something like a city with the queen bee, the male drones and the workers. Every bee has some kind of a job. Some bees tend the baby bees, others take care of the queen bee, som fan air into the hive, and the cleaners keep the hive clean. Then there are the guards for every hive and they sting an enemy that might come too near. Many of the worker bees do nothing but gather nectar for honey. The queen bee does nothing but lay eggs. A honeybee, like other insects, goes through changes from egg to wormlike larva, then the larva becomes a pupa, and finally becomes a full-grown bee.

Baby bees that are to become queens some day are fed with special food which is called royal jelly. If you would like to taste some of this royal jelly, it may be bought at a health-food store—and it tastes good.

The more you learn about bees the more fascinating they become. They are really remarkable insects. One scientist experimented by covering up a bee's eyes and this bee found its way over a distance of two miles back to its home hive.

Men have put bees to work in other ways besides making honey for them. Several times, bees have been used to help win wars, when a commander ordered beehives to be thrown into attacking cavalry. The enraged bees began to sting horses and men. The horses bolted and the soldiers forgot to fight while they ran away from the stinging bees.

There are many kinds of bees. Some, like the honeybees, live together in large numbers. But certain bees are hermits; they prefer to live alone. One of these is the large black variety of the carpenter bee. And this bee does something very unusual—it makes a cake!

First the carpenter bee digs out its nest in a piece of firewood or a fencepost. It has exceptionally strong, sharp jaws, so is equipped by nature to dig into wood and prepare its nursery. Next this bee goes out to hunt food, gathering nectar from the flowers the same as other bees. But here is where the carpenter bee does something different from any other bee; it mixes the flower nectar with some of the pollen from the stamen of the flower. This mixture forms a tiny cake. It is almost like a baker preparing a real cake mixture. Only the bee does not bake the nectar-pollen cake. Instead, she places it into the bottom of the nest. And on top of this cake, she lays an egg.

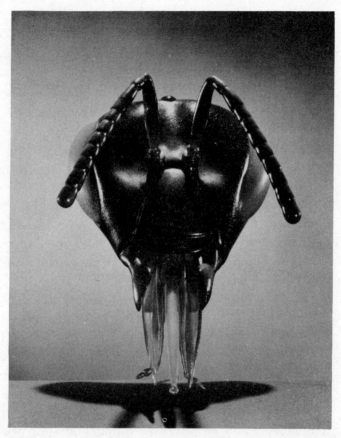

Head of a worker honeybee

After having done this, the carpenter bee takes some of the sawdust that was left when she dug her nest in the wood, and she mixes this with a kind of glue from her own mouth. She then builds a tiny wall of hardened sawdust, covering both the egg and the pollen-nectar bee cake. On top of this sawdust wall another egg is laid and placed alongside a bee cake, until there are many rooms of the nursery inside the log. The mother bee's work is done; her babies will be provided for and she leaves.

These sealed-up eggs hatch into tiny grubs and their food is right next to them—a nice nectar-pollen bee cake. They eat this whenever they are hungry. Soon the grubs change into inactive pupae and finally come out as black carpenter bees.

During all these changes the babies are still sealed up inside their nursery. But when the time comes to leave the nest, the baby bees have a problem—how to get out of the prison-nursery where they are sealed up tight. Up above and all around a baby carpenter bee are still more baby bees. If the one at the bottom wants to get out first there is only one way to do it. The baby must cut its way through all the other rooms of the nursery, using its sharp teeth to bite its way out. It crawls over its brothers and sisters and finally, it is outside in the great big world. What a struggle it had to get there!

CHAPTER 28

Fish Savage and Fish Archer

The archer fish is funny and makes everyone laugh. But the blood-thirsty piranhas that live in the Amazon River of South America fill everyone with terror. No one knows what makes each the way it is, but if you ever decide to have a pet fish, DON'T have a piranha!

Some scientists consider the piranha more dangerous than the shark. They are only tiny fish, ranging from four to eighteen inches in length, but they always travel in large groups and thousands of them attack at one time. Piranhas have been known to tear all the flesh off an animal or human in a few minutes, leaving only a bare skeleton. Their teeth are razor sharp and, for their size, they are one of the most vicious animals on our globe.

Piranha

Piranhas are really pretty little fish, except for their wicked-looking teeth. Some are colored bluish-gray, yellow or green, and spotted with red or gold. Natives and explorers who must travel by boat on the Amazon River are very careful in these waters. There is always danger of the boat's hitting a hidden tree trunk and tipping the occupants overboard. The thought of this happening is enough to make them shudder with horror.

Just the opposite is the archer fish—a cute little East Indian fish that makes everyone laugh. It gets its name because it is able to squirt water at a bug on a leaf, or even squirt at a flying gnat with perfect aim, just like a person skilled in using a bow and arrow. The archer fish is able to knock its victim into the water with the tiny stream it ejects from its mouth. It sees a bug, takes aim and fires! Down falls the surprised victim. An easy way of getting dinner, don't you think?

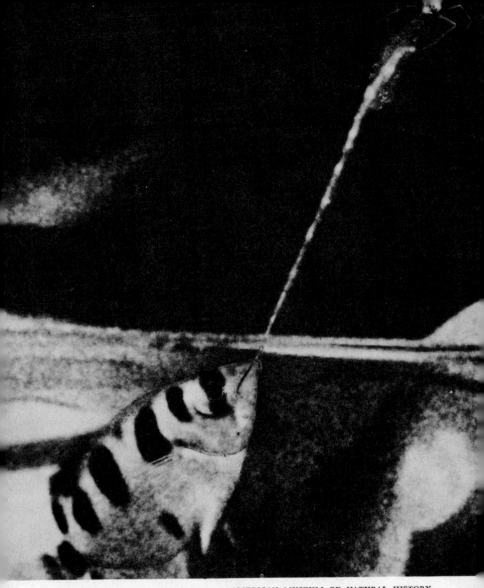

Archer fish

CHAPTER 29

Male Nursemaids

In most animal species it is the female that builds the nest and guards the eggs until they are hatched. But there are some animals that do just the opposite; the male of the species plays nursemaid and often this is done in a most peculiar manner.

The male seahorse has a pouch in his abdomen and the female seahorse deposits in it about two hundred eggs at a time. After fertilizing the eggs, the male carries them around in his pouch for forty days until they hatch. Then his duties end. Both mother and father seahorse leave the newborn babies to take care of themselves.

A seahorse grows only to ten inches in length and gets its name from its horselike head. Instead of scales

Seahorse

a seahorse has a coat of flexible armor, and its body is made up of a series of bony rings. Being a shy fish it spends most of its time clinging upright to underwater weeds with its long tail. Perhaps nature has helped the seahorse to camouflage itself so that it looks more like a weed than a fish because it has no other means of defense against the underwater predators.

Next time you are at the seashore, keep a sharp lookout, and you might find one of these horses of the deep. They are found in all tropical or temperate ocean waters and they are one of the cutest animals of the sea.

Did you ever hear of Darwin's frog? It is a certain species of frog that the great naturalist, Charles Darwin, discovered in the forest of the lower slopes of the Andes. This frog is funny looking with its long, pointed nose, but it does have beautiful yellow and green coloring. Darwin's frog also cares for its eggs in a funny way. After the female lays the eggs the male takes over completely, tending them until they hatch. Then he opens his mouth wide and all the tiny tadpoles enter. No, he does not eat them. He just keeps them in his mouth, protecting and caring for them, until they become complete froglets and are ready to hop around in the outside world. Imagine carrying around a mouth full of squirming tadpoles!

173

Darwin's dwarf frog

Darwin's frog must certainly love its babies a great deal to put up with this discomfort, don't you think so?

There are many kinds of male birds that help in hatching eggs and raising young. Among them is the cuckoo bird found in the American tropics. Several females lay their eggs in nests together, then take turns incubating them. And the males take their turn sitting on the eggs and keeping them warm, too.

Penguins in frozen Antarctica have an unusual way of caring for their children. As soon as the eggs are laid in the nest lined with stones, the male and female penguin take turns incubating them. And when the eggs hatch, both mother and father help care for the chicks. Then, as soon as the babies are half grown, they are placed in "nurseries." About twenty young penguins are cared for by some of the old birds, and all the mothers and fathers go out to hunt for food for themselves and their babies. This is quite a good idea except that the "nursemaids" in charge of the twenty baby penguins must have a hard time caring for all these cute, active youngsters that want to get out of the nursery and see what is going on in the rest of the world.

The stickleback fish is a tiny brackish-water species. When it is time for egg laying and nest building the male uses fibers from water plants and binds them together with a glandular cement that it alone se-

175

cretes. After the female lays the eggs, the tiny male stickleback becomes fierce and savage while guarding them. It will try to tear up other fish ten times its own size if they come near the eggs.

Many fresh- and salt-water fish eggs are guarded by the father fish. The fresh-water bass is one of these. As soon as the female places the eggs in a nest on the bottom of a lake or stream, the male takes over. He "aerates" or fans the eggs with his tail so that they will get plenty of oxygen. But as soon as the baby bass hatch, their father-protector goes off and leaves them entirely to shift for themselves.

If you are a male, don't feel as if you are a sissy because you have to baby-sit some time. Even animals do it!

CHAPTER 30

Odd Primates

Let us take a safari into the jungles of Brazil. We will travel by fast plane for we want to get there and back again quickly in order to cover a lot of territory and see many strange animals.

Our plane makes a safe landing in a clearing of the jungle. We must be alert, for in the thousands of miles of Brazil's tall trees and tangled plant growth, there will be danger. Fierce wild animals prowl through this wild land. There are deadly poisonous snakes and insects. Many natives live in as primitive a way as they did hundreds of years ago. The tribes have many strange customs. In some, fearless hunters smear multicolored paint on their faces and bodies, and witch doctors wear grotesque masks. The Brazil-

Howler monkey

ian jungle is the home of many kinds of primates, but right now we are on the lookout for howler monkeys, the noisiest animals in the world.

Suddenly we hear a terrible din and we look up into the branches of the leafy trees overhead. Dozens of monkeys are leaping from tree to tree. We know by their noise that they are howlers. If one hundred people would yell with blood-curdling sounds as loudly as they could, all at one time, it would sound something like the noise made by howlers—a noise that often fills listeners with terror. The reason they scream so loudly and so often is because they are warning enemies or rival monkey tribes to stay away from their territory. They are really bluffing, for howlers will seldom fight. But anything within ear-shot is usually scared off by their terrible screeching.

Howler monkeys are real acrobats, swinging through the trees at dizzy heights. They seldom stay in one place and always travel in groups, slowly covering about a quarter of a mile a day. If one howler monkey is injured, its distress cries will stop the whole band.

Up in the branches of the trees we see many baby monkeys clinging to their mothers' backs. This whole band is on the move to new feeding grounds and when they are directly overhead the noise is earsplitting.

Then one mama does a strange thing! She has

Gorilla family (painting by Arthur Jansson)

come to a wide gap between two trees that must be crossed, and she knows her half-grown youngster cannot jump that far. Down below, about forty feet, is the hard ground. A fall means certain death. So mama grabs hold of the branches of both trees, then stretches out as flat and straight as she possibly can. She is using her own body to form a living bridge. The young monkey walks over its mother's back, spanning the wide gap that otherwise it would be unable to cross. The howler monkey has proved that she not only has great love for her youngster but that she has brains, as well, to handle certain emergencies.

If we were to make a safari to equatorial Africa we might be lucky enough to see the largest of all primates, the mighty gorilla. Here in the hot, steamy Congo jungle where the gorilla makes its home, we would not be able to stand by and watch, for these great apes want to be left alone. They are usually harmless, but will attack if they or their families are disturbed.

Gorillas live in family groups. There is the male, which has the strength of thirty men, the female, and several children. Often there is a newborn baby gorilla along with the full-grown brothers and sisters.

If you have ever built your own tree house you will know how gorillas sleep at night. They are like gypsy humans in that they roam over the countryside. That is why they must provide a new place to sleep every night. They select a tree and build a platform of branches. Here the female and youngsters sleep while the male stands guard.

A gorilla has a strange habit that frightens everyone—it beats its chest violently. Why does it do this, you will wonder. Simply because it feels well and happy and this is the way it shows it in gorillaland.

In captivity gorillas love candy bars. They will carefully remove the wrapping, eat the candy bar, then squeeze the wrapper into a tiny ball and hide it. In zoos, gorillas learn to love their keepers. But the keepers always stay at arm's length from a gorilla, not because they are afraid of attack, but because they don't want to be *hugged to death* with affection.

Certain primates are trained easily and make excellent pets. They may even be taught to work for man. As far back as 2000 B.C. monkeys were used to help humans with crops. They were especially good at gathering figs and palm fruit. Even today, the macaque, an intelligent monkey, works for man in Malaya and Sumatra. With a cord fastened around its middle the monkey climbs a coconut palm tree. It grabs a coconut and waits for the order from its master as to whether or not the coconut is ripe enough to pick. Then, when given an okay, the monkey twists the coconut around until it breaks off the stem and the nut falls to the ground.

182

There is also another way a monkey was once employed which was not so nice. A chimpanzee, smartest of all the primates, was trained by its owner to be a thief. It would climb into hotel windows and steal anything it was able to carry. Then it would bring the loot back to its master. Of course the owner was caught and sent to jail and the poor, misguided monkey-thief landed in a zoo.

It might surprise you to know about one particular young gorilla that was a pet in a house. As gorillas are very clean animals, it slept in a real bed and loved to take showers. This gorilla even turned the light on and off at night by itself when it was necessary. Now, probably you'll be bringing a baby gorilla home for a pet instead of a dog!

Tailpiece

You do not have to be a scientist to find out strange things about the animal world. Many important discoveries have been made by laymen who have had no training at all. So why not be an amateur scientist and solve some of the exciting mysteries in the animal kingdom? You could be an amateur ichthyologist, a scientist who studies fish, or an entomologist, a scientist who studies insects, or a zoologist, a scientist who studies animals. You could investigate, yourself, some of the strange animals of our world—at the seashore, in the woods, and even in the vacant lot nearby and in your own yard.

Don't kill harmless animals. Instead, *observe* them. Keep your eyes open and your ears alert when near animals. You might make an important contribution to the human race by discovering medicines or by-products derived from animals or something else of value to our generation and generations to come.

Here is one idea! In the Florida Keys are miniature deer, about one-half the size of whitetailed deer. These tiny deer swim from island to island and are very wild and extremely timid. No one knows how they got there or why they are so small. Perhaps, if you were the one who found out the reason these deer are so small, while all other deer are normally sized, it might be a key to controlling growth. We might, at will, regulate growth so that we have giant cattle which would produce thousands of pounds of meat. And, if a circus elephant became unruly, it could be reduced to miniature size and locked up in a bird cage until it got over its rampage.

If growth could be controlled, you might think about still another idea—to make aphids grow as big as cows and ants as big as people. Then we could have honeydew dairies. The ants would be working for us, milking the aphids, and all we would have to do is go to the ant barns and gather up the sweet substance.

Even if you never do make important discoveries you might just have fun and see funny things if you *observe* animals. Like the man watching a rat—he noticed that the rat was carrying its own tail to its nest. Silly creature!

There are about a million kinds of animals known to man. No one knows how many more have *not* been discovered. Up on high, icy mountain ranges or in caves inside our earth or in ocean depths may be living even stranger animals than some already known. Perhaps *you* might be the one to find a tiny fish or a giant mammal never before seen by man, a living fossil of prehistoric times.

If you want to learn from animals or to make discoveries of new kinds of animals, you should *protect* them. And in order to protect animals one of the main rules is to protect the forests, for trees, plants and flowers mean shelter and food for wildlife. *Don't* start a fire accidentally, for a tiny flame may grow to an enormous blaze, burning and destroying acres and miles of growth. Many animals will be destroyed along with plants and trees that took years to grow. So be careful when you have a campfire or any kind of flame in wooded areas.

Another important way to protect wildlife is to protect water, for water is so important to animals that all wildlife may become extinct in a certain area if water holes, lakes or streams dry up. *You* can help this situation, too, by not wasting water. Even though water is never used up—it rains, sinks into the earth, reaches an underground stream, then comes to earth's surface in a flowing well or lake—the water you let soak into the ground and be wasted may go so far below that it could take hundreds of years for it to be used by man again.

If you want to observe animals, if you want to learn from animals—SAVE WOODLANDS, SAVE WATER, SAVE WILDLIFE—all of which means CONSERVATION.

And if you do happen to make strange discoveries about animals, you might find it to be just as exciting as taking a jet trip to the moon.

187

INDEX